Energy Law in Mexico

Energy Law in Mexico

Third Edition

Jose Juan Gonzalez

This book was originally published as a monograph in the International Encyclopaedia of Laws/Energy Law.

Founding Editor: Roger Blanpain
General Editor: Frank Hendrickx
Volume Editors: Kurt Deketelaere & Bram Delvaux

Wolters Kluwer

Published by:
Kluwer Law International B.V.
PO Box 316
2400 AH Alphen aan den Rijn
The Netherlands
E-mail: lrs-sales@wolterskluwer.com
Website: www.wolterskluwer.com/en/solutions/kluwerlawinternational

Sold and distributed by:
Wolters Kluwer Legal & Regulatory U.S.
7201 McKinney Circle
Frederick, MD 21704
United States of America
E-mail: customer.service@wolterskluwer.com

ISBN 978-94-035-1646-2

e-Book: ISBN 978-94-035-1196-2
web-PDF: ISBN 978-94-035-1206-8

The Author

Professor Jose Juan Gonzalez (born, 1959), who holds a Juris Doctor Degree (Mexico, 1981), an LLM in Economic Law (Mexico, 1984) and a PhD in Environmental Law (Spain, 1999), is a full Professor and Researcher at the Metropolitan Autonomous University in Mexico. In addition to research and scientific service, he teaches courses Property of Natural Resources, Tax Law and Environmental Law. He is also the Chairman of the Mexican Institute for Environmental Law Research and Director of the *Mexican Environmental Law Journal*. Professor Gonzalez is a fellow of the National Research System of the Mexican Council of Science and Technology. He was also a member of the Governing Council of the UICN Academy of Environmental Law and of the Academic Advisory Group of the International Bar Association, Energy, Environment and Infrastructure Law section.

In the past, he was Director of the Legal Division of the Attorney General's Office for Environmental Protection. Professor Gonzalez is the author of several books and articles in the fields of Latin American and Mexican Environmental Law, Tax Law and Energy Law. Besides his academic activities, he is an adviser for a number of federal and local governmental agencies in the field of environmental enforcement and compliance. In 1999, he drafted the currently in force Environmental Act of Mexico City.

Professor Gonzalez is also a member of the editorial boards of the *Energy and Natural Resources Law Journal*, the *Macquarie Journal of International and Comparative Environmental Law* and the *Revista do direito ambiental*. In 2008, he organized the Sixth Annual Colloquium of the UICN Academy of Environmental Law.

The Author

Table of Contents

List of Abbreviations

AGEP	Attorney General for Environmental Protection
AGOEP	Attorney General Office for Environmental Protection
BEM	*Basis of Electricity Market*
CCGL	Climate Change General Law of 2012
CECs	Clean Energy Certificates
ETL	Energy Transition Law of 2015
FCE	Federal Commission of Electricity
FTA	Free Trade Agreement
GDP	Gross Domestic Product
GWEC	Global Wind Energy Council
IMCCC	Inter-Ministerial Commission on Climate Change
LAC	Latin America and the Caribbean
LEI	Law of the Electricity Industry
MAC	Ministry of Administrative Control
ME	Ministry of Energy
MENRF	Ministry of Environment, Natural Resources and Fishing
NAAEC	North American Side-Agreement on Environmental Cooperation
NAISEPES	National Agency of Industrial Security and Environmental Protection for Energy Sector
NCCNG	National Centre for Control of Natural Gas
NCEC	National Centre of Energy Control
NCEUE	National Commission for an Efficient Use of Energy
NCH	National Commission of Hydrocarbons
NCNSS	National Commission of Nuclear Security and Safeguards
NDP	National Development Plan
NWA	National Water Act
NWC	National Waters Commission
OPEC	Organization of Petroleum Exporting Countries
ORM	Operational Rules of the Market

List of Abbreviations

PEMEX	Mexican Petroleum Company
RCE	Regulatory Commission of Energy
ROW	Right of Way
SCJN	Supreme Court of Justice of the Nation
TPP	Trans-Pacific Partnership

Legislation

Forest Act	General Act for Sustainable Forest Development
Environmental Act	General Law of Ecological Equilibrium and Environmental Protection
LCRAEM	Law of Coordinated Regulatory Agencies in Energy Matters
HL	Hydrocarbons Law
EIL	Electricity Industry Law
LPCC	Light and Power of the Centre Company
LPES	Law of the Public Electricity Service
LRH	Law of Revenue from Hydrocarbons
MONs	Mexican Official Norms
NAFTA	North American Free Trade Agreement
RA27CFP	Regulatory Act of Article 27 of the Constitution in the Field of Petroleum
RM	Rules of the Market

Preface

This monograph provides an updated overview of Mexican law and regulations regarding the energy sector and environmental legislation governing it. The document also surveys the historical development of the energy sector legal regime from 1917 to 2021. From such a historical perspective, the study discusses the constitutional reform of 2013 and secondary legislation passed by the Federal Congress in 2014 that made possible private participation in the energy sector under legal certainty basis. In the same vein, the monograph discusses the recent legal changes boosted by the new government to re-establish the state monopoly over the energy sector. The study focuses on analysing the property regimen of energy resources, the regimen of private investment in the energy sector, the legal regime of renewable sources, and the environmental impacts of the energy sector.

The analysis also discusses the Mexican Energy Policy drafted by the National Development Plan (NDP) and programmes under it and the role of governmental agencies in regulating the energy sector.

General Introduction

§1. General Background

1. Until 2013, Mexico was one of the few countries around the world where the state maintained a dominant position in the energy market. However, as discussed in this monograph, international commitments undertaken by the Mexican government, particularly in the North American Free Trade Agreement (NAFTA) (signed and ratified in 1994), had brought the result that, without changing the Constitution, since the 1990s, secondary legislation gradually opened possibilities for private investment in the energy sector.

2. In the case of oil, although there was no possibility of direct participation of the private sector in the activities of exploration, exploitation, production and refining of oil, performing these activities by individuals was possible through the so-called *contracts of multiple services* incorporated into RA27CFP by reform of 2008. *Multiple services contracts* allowed private corporations to carry out – on behalf of the state – all activities reserved to PEMEX (Mexican Petroleum Company) by the Constitution and secondary legislation.

3. Meanwhile, in the case of electricity, although the Mexican State maintained the role of a single buyer and unique distributor, it was not the only generator, for the Law of the Public Electricity Service (LPES) as amended in 1992 allowed the generation of electricity by private entities under the various legal mechanism, such as self-generation,[1] cogeneration[2] and independent production.[3]

4. However, full incorporation of private investment – national and foreign – in the energy sector required greater legal certainty that only could be achieved through a constitutional amendment. In that direction, both the Federal and local

1. Consists of an enterprise of another party that may acquire, establish and/or operate an electrical generating facility in Mexico to meet the enterprise's own needs.
2. Consists of an enterprise of another party that may acquire, establish and/or operate a cogeneration facility in Mexico that generates electricity using heat, steam or other energy sources associated with an industrial process. Owners of the industrial facility need not be the owners of the cogenerating facility.
3. Consists of an enterprise of another party that may acquire, establish and/or operate an electricity generation facility for independent power production in Mexico.

congresses passed the constitutional energy reform in December 2013. To complement such constitutional amendment, in 2014, the Federal Congress passed nine new legal bodies and reformed another twelve.

5. Under the new constitutional and legal framework, the Mexican Energy Sector started two major simultaneous transformations. The first consisted of opening the energy sector to private investment,[4] while the second addressed promoting more significant participation of clean energies within the energy matrix.[5]

6. In that context, the Constitutional reform in energy matters of 2013 drove the Mexican energy sector's liberalization. The new energy laws passed in 2014[6] and other legal bodies relating to the energy sector approved in the same year established the legal mechanisms addressed to get that aim.[7]

7. The constitutional reform also concerned the energy transition. Even when Articles 25, 26 and 27, as amended in 2013, did not refer to renewables, transitory Articles 16, 18 and 19 of the amendment provided a specific foundation to more relevant participation of clean energies into the energy matrix.[8] Under such a constitutional basis, in 2014, the Federal Congress passed the Geothermal Energy Law.

---

4. According to one author, there are two reasons for this energy transition. On the one hand, the process of climate change. On the other hand, the physical limits that characterize fossil energy sources, as oil, gas, and coal reserves were beginning to run out. Martínez Camarero C, & López V, 'Transición Energética Y Productiva Justa: ¿De Qué Estamos Hablando?' [2015] *Daphnia* <http://www.daphnia.es/revista/63/articulo/1242/Transicion-energetica-y-productiva-justa-de-que-estamos-hablando> accessed 9 Mar. 2021).
5. According to Vaclav Smil, the energy transition is a gradual change in the way an economy procures the primary energy it needs to function. Villareal and Tornel point out that energy transition is the process that transforms a centralized, fossil fuel-dependent energy system into a decentralized, environmentally more sustainable, low-carbon, and socially more inclusive system, Villareal J, & Tornel C, *La Transición Energética En México: Retos Y Oportunidades Para Una Política Ambientalmente Sustentable Y Socialmente Inclusiva* (Fundación Friedrich-Ebert-Stiftung 2017).
6. The new laws are: (1) Law on Hydrocarbons; (2) Law on the Electricity Industry; (3) Law on Geothermal Energy; (4) Law on the Coordinated Regulatory Bodies in Energy Matters; (5) Law on the National Agency for Industrial Safety and Environmental Protection in the Hydrocarbons Sector; (6) Law on Petróleos Mexicanos; (7) Law on the Federal Electricity Commission; (8) Law on Hydrocarbon Revenues, and (9) Law on the Mexican Petroleum Fund for Stabilization and Development. All these laws were published in the Official Journal of the Federation on 11 Aug. 2014.
7. The laws that were reformed are (1) Law on National Waters; (2) Organic Law of the Federal Public Administration; (3) Law on Foreign Investment; (4) Mining Law; (5) Law on Public-Private Partnerships; (6) Federal Law on Parastatal Entities; (7) Law on Procurement; Leasing; and Public Sector Services; (8) Law on Public Works and Related Services; (9) Federal Law on Duties; (10) Law on Fiscal Coordination; Federal Law on Budget and Fiscal Responsibility; and (11) General Law on Public Debt. All these reforms were published in the Official Journal of the Federation on 11 Aug. 2014.
8. The Electricity Industry Law of 2014 (EIL) was designed to 'promote the sustainable development of the electricity industry and to guarantee its continuous, efficient and safe operation for the benefit of users, as well as compliance with principles of public and universal service, clean energies and pollutant emission reduction obligations'; this law contains just an incipient regulation on clean energies promotion.

The transition towards a low-carbon economy was also a concern shared by the Climate Change General Law of 2012 (CCGL)[9] and the Energy Transition Law of 2015 (ETL).[10] In this regard, one of the objectives of the CCGL is to promote the transition to a competitive, sustainable, and low-carbon economy resilient to extreme hydro-meteorological events associated with climate change.[11] In the same direction, the ETL pursues promoting a progressive increase of clean energies in the electricity industry. In CCGL, Mexico committed to reducing its carbon emissions by 30% in 2020 and 50% in 2050.[12] ETL assumed increasing clean energies by 25% in 2018, 30% in 2021, and 35% in 2024.[13]

8. The double energy transition described above was beginning to deliver results. According to the Clean Energy Progress Report, by the end of the first half of 2018, generation from clean sources had reached 23.4%, less than 2 percentage points below the 25% clean energy generation target established by the Mexican government in the ETL and CCGL.[14] Clean technologies that showed the highest growth were photovoltaic, wind, and cogeneration.[15]

9. However, before the two previous transformations consolidated, a third transformation of the energy sector began to occur. The new government that took the chair at the end of 2018 established as one of the cornerstones of its government strategy, the rescue of energy sovereignty through the re-foundation and strengthening of the public monopolies on the electricity and hydrocarbons industries (Federal Commission of Electricity (FCE) and PEMEX, respectively). This policy is not in line with neither Mexico's commitments before the international community nor the currently in force national energy legal framework.

§2. Mexican Policy Regarding Energy Sector

10. The NDP 2019–2024 clearly describes the renationalization of the energy sector boosted by the government that took the chair in 2018.[16] The NDP points out various arguments that justify that rescue: (a) the energy reform imposed by the previous regimes caused severe damages to PEMEX and FCE; (b) over the past six years, oil production has fallen so steadily that Mexico has gone from being an exporter to an importer of crude oil and refined fuels; and (c) the total output of the

9. Published in the Official Journal of the Federation on 6 Jun. 2012.
10. Published in the Official Journal of the Federation on 24 Dec. 2015.
11. Article two, s. VII of the Climate Change Law.
12. Second Transitory Provision of Climate Change Law.
13. Third transitory Provision of Energy transition Law.
14. Secretaría de Energía, 'Reporte De Avance De Las Energías Limpias. Primer Semestre De 2018' (SENER 2018) <https://www.gob.mx/cms/uploads/attachment/file/418391/RAEL_Primer_Semestre_2018.pdf> accessed 9 Mar. 2021.
15. Update of the Transition Strategy to Promote the Use of Cleaner Technologies and Fuels, published in the Official Journal of the Federation on 7 Feb. 2020.
16. Published in the Official Journal of the Federation on 12 Aug. 2019.

private entities was insignificant, despite the advantageous conditions under which they received the corresponding concessions.

11. The NDP stresses as a strategic purpose of energy policy that, as in the twentieth century, PEMEX and FCE should again operate as levers of national development. To achieve this objective, the plan states that it is necessary to rehabilitate Mexico's six existing refineries, which, according to the document, are in a deplorable situation of abandonment and looting.[17]

12. The plan also envisages the construction of a new refinery and the modernization of state-owned electricity generation facilities. It is important to note that the NDP refers mainly to thermoelectric plants that operate with coal, fuel oil, and gas and are therefore highly polluting.

13. Regarding clean energies, the NDP only refers to hydroelectric power plants[18] and states that these, together with the old thermoelectric plants,[19] will receive additional resources for their modernization. Wind and solar energies are not in the perspective of the 4th Transformation's energy policy.

14. In addition to the above, the only reference that the NDP includes to the decarbonization of the energy matrix is in the sense of stating 'the new energy policy of the Mexican State will promote sustainable development through the incorporation of populations and communities to the production of energy with renewable sources'.[20]

15. In line with the NDP, although formally the constitutional reform of 2013 and its secondary laws of 2014 have not been repealed, in practice, energy reform was halted and began to be reversed almost immediately after the start of the new presidential term.

16. The new government is moving forward on the NDP's terms in two ways. On the one hand, it reversed the energy transition, and, on the other, it is trying to take PEMEX and FCE's competitors out of the market. However, as both the constitutional reform of 2013 and the new secondary legislation of 2014 are still in force, the energy policy designed by the NDP resulted in illegal.

---

17. Six refineries currently operate in Mexico: Salamanca, Guanajuato; Minatitlán, Veracruz; Tula, Hidalgo; Cadereyta, Nuevo León; Salina Cruz, Oaxaca; and Ciudad Madero, Tamaulipas.
18. There are currently sixty-four hydroelectric power plants in Mexico, all of them under the control of the Federal Electricity Commission (Comisión Federal de Electricidad). Twenty are large, forty-four are small. Fifty-seven produce electricity and seven are out of operation. Ramos-Gutiérrez and Montenegro-Fragoso (2012).
19. There are thirty thermoelectric plants in the country.
20. Official Journal of the Federation, 'Plan Nacional De Desarrollo 2019-2024' (2019) http://dof.gob.mx/nota_detalle.php?codigo=5565599&fecha=12/07/2019.

§3. CONSTITUTIONAL PRINCIPLES RULING ENERGY POLICY AND LAW

17. The Mexican Constitution establishes the principles that should govern energy policies and law.

18. In line with paragraph 4 of Article 27 of the Constitution, petroleum, and solid, liquid, or gaseous hydrocarbons, into the subsoil are the nation's property, and no concessions to private parties for its exploitation are allowed. However, the Constitution separates the different stages of the energy sector into strategic and non-strategic activities. According to paragraph 7 of Article 27, exploration and exploitation of hydrocarbons are strategic activities reserved for the estate, while the rest of the activities of the hydrocarbons industry are open to private investment. Notwithstanding the preceding, the nation may carry out strategic activities through assignments granted to productive state corporations or through the signing of contracts for private companies.

19. Regarding the electricity industry, paragraph 6 of Article 27 of the Constitution also separates strategic activities from non-strategic ones. By the mentioned provision, planning and control of the National Electricity System and transmission and distribution of electricity are strategic activities reserved for the nation. In contrast, activities of generation and supply of electricity are open to private investment.

20. Finally, in line with paragraph 8 of Article 27, only the nation can use nuclear fuels to produce atomic energy and regulate their use for other purposes.

21. On the other hand, the Mexican Constitution does not refer to renewable sources of energy, but Article 25 introduces a few principles addressed to guarantee the sustainability of the energy sector. In this regard, Article 25 of the Constitution decrees that: 'direction of national development belongs to the State to guarantee that it is integral and sustainable' and also that:

> under specific criteria of social equity, productivity and sustainability, there will be support and impulse for enterprises from the social and private sectors of the economy, subjecting them to the modalities dictated by public interests and to the usage for the general benefit of the productive resources, while taking care of its preservation and the environment.

22. In the same direction, Article 4 of the Mexican Constitution establishes the right of all people to a healthy environment for their development and well-being. This provision also holds that environmental degradation and damage will generate liability for those who provoke it regarding what the law provides. Consequently, the energy sector activities must be carried out in a way that does not affect that human rights.

23. The Constitution also deals with the financial aspects of the energy sector. In this sense, Articles 26 and 28 establish the foundation for the operation of productive state corporations as the entities in charge of operating the strategic areas described above and compete with private corporations in non-strategic areas.

24. In addition, Article 28 of the Constitution creates the Mexican Petroleum Fund for Stability and Development as a trust in charge of managing oil revenues. To avoid political management of this income, the Constitution indicates that the Central Bank administers the Fund.

25. Consequently, according to the currently described constitutional principles, activities of the energy sector are divided into strategic and non-strategic. Transmission and distribution are strategic activities in the electricity industry, whereas generation and supply are open to private investment. In the hydrocarbons industry, exploration and exploitation are strategic, while refining and supply are open to private investment. Besides, criteria of sustainability and environmental protection govern the energy sector.

§4. Sources of Energy Law

I. International Sources

26. Mexican energy policy is limited by what the international trade treaties signed by Mexico provide. The Supreme Court of Justice of the Nation (SCJN) has indicated that the International Treaties are at the same hierarchical level as the Constitution but, when such treaties protect human rights, they complement constitutional provisions. Therefore, the provisions of these treaties on energy matters determine the content of the Mexican energy legislation. In the following sections, we will analyse the content of international energy law from three points of view: from the energy point of thought itself; from the perspective of international trade treaties; and finally, from the arena of environmental law.

A. International Energy Treaties

27. As Heftye points out, unlike what happens with other branches of public international law, in energy law, voluntary agreements are concluded between states and transnational companies, so that these agreements are not considered as international treaties.[21] However, members of the international community have signed international agreements that led to the creation of international organizations in the energy sector. Among these organizations we can mention: the Organization of Petroleum Exporting Countries (OPEC) that was created in 1960 to unify policies

21. Heftye Etienne, F. Las fuentes del Derecho Internacional Energético. available at https://goo.gl/1ueQuE.

on oil prices; the International Energy Agency, created in 1974 to promote cooperation between oil-importing countries; the International Atomic Energy Agency created in 1957 to establish and manage nuclear energy safeguards; the Organization of Arab Petroleum Exporting Countries created in 1968 to coordinate policies among Arab nations; the Latin American Energy Organisation that was established in 1973 with the objective of promoting the integration, conservation, rational use, commercialization, and defence of the energy resources of the region; and, the Latin American Regional Petroleum Alliance established in 1967.[22] Mexico does not belong to OPEC, but under a collaboration agreement signed in 2016, it participates in the OPEC plus group. However, since 2018, it has been a member of the International Energy Agency and since 1958 it has been a member of the International Atomic Energy Agency and the Latin American Energy Organisation since 1975.

B. *Commercial Treatises*

1. The NAFTA

28. The NAFTA signed by Mexico, the United States, and Canada in 1992[23] led to Mexico's energy sector reorganization. In ANNEX 620(3) to Chapter Six of NAFTA, Mexico entered several reservations on strategic activities that concern, among others, the trade and investment in the energy sector. However, some exemptions to this reservation are possible.[24] The Mexican State reserves the right to supply electricity as a public service in Mexico, including generation, transmission, transformation, distribution, and electricity supply. Per NAFTA, Mexico does not permit private investment in energy sector activities, except under the conditions provided in Annex 602(3) paragraph 5.[25] The Annex lists the following areas: production for own use, cogeneration and independent power production.

29. In line with Annex 602(3), activities and investment in electricity generation facilities permissible are the productions for own uses and cogeneration of electricity using energy sources associated with an industrial process.

30. Own use producers must sell their surplus of electricity production to FCE. Besides, independent power producers (IPP) located in Mexico are obliged to sell all generated electricity to the FCE, which is obligated to buy such electricity under terms and conditions agreed with the IPP. IPPs located in Mexico are allowed to export electricity to other NAFTA parties.

---

22. Elizarrás JCV, El nuevo derecho internacional de la energía a través del estatuto de sus fuentes y el ordenamientos del mercado mundial del petróleo en un contexto especulativo. Anuaria Mexicano de Derecho Internacional, vol. 9 Ciudad de México, January, 2009.
23. NAFTA came into force on 1 Jan. 1994.
24. Horlick G, and Schuchhardt C, *NAFTA Provisions and Electricity Sector* (Commission for Environmental Cooperation of North America 2002).
25. *Ibid.*

31. Despite its reservation of the right to supply and the conditions imposed on Mexico's investment by electricity producers from NAFTA countries, Mexico does not prohibit electricity imports by NAFTA suppliers. Mexico has entered exceptions to Article 603 on import and export restrictions. Under these exemptions, Mexico may restrict the granting of import and export licences in certain goods listed in the Annex. Market access, however, is limited due to the reservations on the distribution of electricity established by Annex 602(3) since the importer of electricity will likely have to sell directly to FCE.[26]

32. As a result of NAFTA's negotiations, in 1992, the Mexican Congress reformed the Public Service of Electricity Law.[27] The reform allowed domestic and foreign private investment in small-scale production, the export of electricity from cogeneration, import of energy exclusively for own use, and generation of power for emergency use. The reform also allowed the participation of independent electricity producers for exclusive sale to FCE. Due to NAFTA, the electricity industry organization in Mexico changed from a state monopoly model vertically integrated into all industry phases to a single buyer model. NAFTA did not include specific rules on private investment in the hydrocarbons industry.

33. In NAFTA's case, an amendment to the Public Service Electricity Law incorporated into the national legal system the trade agreement commitments assumed by Mexico. The United States, Mexico and Canada Free Trade Agreement (USMCA) substituted NAFTA in 2020.

34. In contrast, the Trans-Pacific Partnership (TPP) embodies the 2013 energy reform in the text of Annex I of the trade agreement.

2. The TPP

35. The Comprehensive and Progressive Treaty of Trans-Pacific Partnership (TPP) is a free trade agreement (FTA) between several countries in the Pacific agreed on 5 October 2015 after years of hard negotiations in Auckland, New Zealand. The TPP seeks to lower trade barriers, establish a joint intellectual property framework, reinforce environmental standards of labour law, and establish a dispute arbitration mechanism. Per TPP Mexico has permitted foreign participation in its energy sector for the first time. In the TPP, Mexico included several specific energy-related reservations. Such reservations allow foreign investment in the Mexican energy industry under the conditions set out by the constitutional reform

26. *Ibid.*
27. Published in the Official Journal of the Federation on 23 Dec. 1992.

of 2013, excluding any less favourable treatment.[28] Thus, Mexico can liberalize foreign investment restrictions established by the mentioned energy reforms and Annex I without violating the TPP (incorporated through Article 32.11), but it cannot make the rules more restrictive.

36. It means that the United States and Canada, as USMCA members, must receive treatment in the energy sector that is no less favourable than Mexico's accord to the other TPP members, even though the United States did not ratify TPP.[29] The Mexican government cannot make the rules under which foreign investment is allowed in the energy sector more restrictive than those set out in the TPP annexes.

3. The USMCA

37. The USMCA is a FTA between Canada, the United States, and Mexico. The USMCA is the result of the renegotiation of NAFTA proposed by the United States, and after several months of negotiations, the parties signed it on 30 November 2018, as a side event of the 2018 G20 Summit in Buenos Aires.

38. Unlike NAFTA, the USMCA does not have a specific energy chapter.[30] However, different branches of the Agreement contain references to the energy sector.[31]

39. Chapter 8 of USMCA recognizes the Mexican State property over hydrocarbons. This property is direct, inalienable, and imprescriptible. This chapter holds:

> In the case of Mexico, and without prejudice to their rights and remedies available under this Agreement, the United States and Canada recognise that: (a) Mexico reserves its sovereign right to reform its Constitution and its domestic legislation; and (b) Mexico has the direct, inalienable, and imprescriptible ownership of all hydrocarbons in the subsoil of the national territory, including the continental shelf and the exclusive economic zone located outside the territorial sea and adjacent thereto, in strata or deposits, regardless of their physical conditions pursuant to Mexico's Constitution.

---

28. Mexican energy reform of 2013 is directly incorporated into CPTPP Annex I-Mexico (page 17) through Annex I-Mexico (page 27).
29. TPP negotiations concluded on 5 Oct. 2015. It is not a traditional free trade agreement; it is a form of 'economic constitution' that provides the foundational rules for the governance of cross-border trade and investment in the Pacific region.
30. This agreement replaced the North American Free Trade Agreement (NAFTA), which in 1994 created the world's largest free-trade region. The new Free Trade Agreement between Mexico, the United States, and Canada, known as USMCA, came into force On 1 Jul. 2020.
31. For their part, Canada and the United States negotiated a side letter to the USMCA on energy. Letter from Robert Lighthizer to Chrystia Freeland (30 Nov. 2018) <https://www.international.gc.ca/trade-commerce/assets/pdfs/agreements-accords/cusma-aceum/letter-energy.pdf>accessed 6 Feb. 2020.

40. However, Chapter 8 does not provide the basis for an energy policy that prevents private investment in the energy sector. There are other constraints in the USMCA to modify energy industry structure beyond those included in Chapter 8.[32] Mexico accepts in the USMCA a kind of 'most favoured nation' clause, agreeing to grant other parties a treatment on energy that is no more restrictive than that Mexico grants to parties of other trade agreements Mexico has concluded. The key USMCA provision is as follows: 'Article 32.11: Specific Provision on Cross-Border Trade in Services, Investment, and Productive State Corporations and Designated Monopolies for Mexico.'

41. Concerning the obligations in Chapter 14 (Investment), Chapter 15 (Cross-Border Trade in Services), and Chapter 22 (Productive State Corporations and Designated Monopolies), Mexico reserves the right to adopt or maintain a measure for a sector or sub-sector 32-12 for which Mexico has not taken a specific reservation in its Schedules to Annexes I, II, and IV of this agreement, only to the extent consistent with the least restrictive measures that Mexico may adopt or maintain under the terms of applicable reservations and exceptions to parallel obligations in other trade and investment agreements that Mexico has ratified before entry into force of this Agreement, including the World Trade Organization (WTO) Agreement, without regard to whether those other agreements have entered into force.

42. Under this clause, Mexico must afford treatment to the Canadian and United States investors in sectors covered by the three chapters of USMCA listed in Article 32.11 that is no less favourable than Mexico's treatment in parallel trade and investment agreements. This clause refers to the rules established by the TPP. Therefore, in general terms, the USMCA locks in Mexico's energy reform.

4. The FTA Between Mexico and the European Union

43. On 30 September 2000, the Economic Partnership, Political Coordination and Cooperation Agreement between the United Mexican States and the European Community and its Member States entered into force. The Economic Partnership, Political Coordination and Cooperation Agreement between the United Mexican States and the European Community and its Member States protects European investment in the Mexican energy sector due to the *parity principle*.[33]

44. Two Chapters of NAFTA established the possibility of participation of foreign companies in the domestic electricity industry. Like many other clauses, these chapters automatically apply to the EU-Mexico FTA based on the principle 'NAFTA parity'. NAFTA parity means matching the benefits that NAFTA offered in terms of liberalization of capital and commodities, under terms that could be

32. Gantz D, *The United States-Mexico Canada Agreement: Energy Production and Policies* (Rice University's Baker Institute for Public Policy 2019) <https://www.bakerinstitute.org/media/files/files/a7b744b6/bi-report-091719-mex-usmca-5.pdf> accessed 9 Mar. 2021.
33. Adopted on 16 Jun. 2000.

similar or better than those established in NAFTA but never inferior.[34] The European Union (EU) achieved through the EU-Mexico FTA the same treatment and similar relief conditions Mexico granted to the United States and Canada under NAFTA. Mexico should recognize to EU any future preferences given to NAFTA members.

45. The same rule applies to USMCA. This commercial treaty has already repealed NAFTA, but the *parity principle* also applies to the rules established by the TPP. In other words, given that the TPP is part of the Mexican energy reform, it is impossible to modify either the United Mexican States' Political Constitution or the law to prevent European companies' participation without confronting the trade dispute settlement system provided by the trade treaties between Mexico and the EU. Recently Mexico and the EU renegotiated the FTA. Negotiations finished in 2020. The text of the new Agreement ratifies the principle of parity.

46. Currently, trade relations between the EU and Mexico are governed by the trade pillar of the EU-Mexico Economic Partnership, Political Coordination and Cooperation Agreement. This Agreement came into force in 2020.

C. The International Environmental Law

47. Mexico committed in the Paris Agreement that 35% of the energy generated by 2024, and 43% by 2030, would be clean. These targets and others, such as reducing short-lived greenhouse gases by 25% and black carbon emissions by 51%, require incentives.[35]As previously mentioned, the 2013 energy reform brought Mexico closer to these goals, but the government that took the chair in 2018 halted such an energy transition.

48. One of the critical elements to meet the targets is to generate economic mechanisms to produce clean energy. To this end, Mexico designed three auctions between 2015 and 2017, resulting in ninety contracts equivalent to an investment of USD 9 billion to develop solar, wind and geothermal energy. These projects would reduce emissions by 54 million tonnes of CO_2 by 2030. Mexico was moving in the right direction, but everything changed in 2018.

49. The new government energy policy postulates the return to a carbon-based economy. The idea of building a new refinery and rehabilitating the six old ones

34. This equalization stems from a bill that was extensively debated during five legislative periods in the US Congress between 1995 and 2002. The initiative, known as the Caribbean Basin Interim Trade Program/NAFTA Parity, was passed by both chambers and signed by President Clinton on 18 May 2000, and authorized for implementation on 2 Oct. 2000 in Presidential Proclamation 7351. Gutierrez Haces M, 'Incidencia Del TLCAN y De Los Acuerdos De Protecci6n A La Inversi6n Extranjera Sobre Las Relaciones De México Con La Uni6n Europea' (2014) Economía UNAM

35. Nevertheless, the Mexican government has recently launched two projects that directly contradict the Paris agreement: the construction of a refinery in Dos Bocas, Tabasco, and a thermoelectric plan in Huexca, Morelos.

illustrates this argument. The various measures aimed at strengthening FCE and PEMEX position in the energy market also reflect the government's nostalgia for Mexico's oil boom years. Consequently, while the whole world is transitioning to a low-carbon economy, Mexico is trying to return to a carbon-based economy. Perhaps one of the most questionable steps backwards that the government has taken is modifying the rules to grant clean energy certificates (CECs).

50. As analysed, the reform to Energy Industry Law (EIL) of 2021 allows the Ministry of Energy (ME) to grant CECs for old power plants that the FCE already had in operation before the regulation that endorsed the use of these instruments came into force in 2014.[36] This legal change indicates that Mexico has given up on its international commitments to clean energy and climate change. However, during the Major Economies Energy and Climate Forum held in June 2022, the president of Mexico announced ten of Mexico's commitments for climate change. Some of them contradict the objectives of the 2021 EIL reform, whereas others seem to be in line with the idea of maintaining Mexico in a scheme of a carbon-based economy. The commitments are:

(1) Project to modernize sixteen hydroelectric plants.
(2) Pemex investment of USD 2 billion with the objective of reducing methane gas emissions by up to 98%.
(3) Commitment to produce 50% of zero-emission vehicles by 2030.
(4) Construction of Photovoltaic Solar Park in Puerto Peñasco, Sonora.
(5) Investment by seventeen US companies in Mexico to produce solar and wind energy.
(6) Creation of solar parks on the US-Mexico border and transmission grids to export electricity to California and other US entities.
(7) Modernization of the six refineries located in Mexico.
(8) Construction of coker plants in Tula, Hidalgo and Salina Cruz, Oaxaca.
(9) Implementation of the most important reforestation programme in the world, with the planting of 1 million hectares of fruit and timber trees.
(10) Commitment to produce at least 35% of all energy from clean and renewable sources by 2024.

II. National Sources

51. Because of Mexican Constitutional Energy Reform of 2013 secondary legislation was almost totally transformed. As previously mentioned, nine new laws were passed by the Federal Congress and other eleven were amended in 2014. In addition, in 2015, the Federal Congress passed the Energy Transition Law. So, the new Mexican Energy Law is composed of those laws that were enacted before the

36. The document highlights that, since 2019, Mexico is the second country that allocates more subsidies to fossil fuels, after China as it has allocated USD 17 billion in subsidies to fossil fuels such as oil and gas, mainly through Petróleos Mexicanos and the Federal Electricity Commission.

constitutional reform but were not repealed by it and those new laws were passed as a consequence of the constitutional amendment.

52. Mexican energy laws currently in force are:

- Law of Hydrocarbons and its regulation;
- Law of Electric Industry and its regulation;
- Law of Energy Transition;
- Law of Geothermic Energy;
- Law of Coordinated Regulatory Agencies in the Field of Energy;
- Law of the National Agency of Industrial Security and Environmental Protection for the Hydrocarbons Sector;
- Law of the Mexican Petroleum Company;
- Law of the Federal Commission of Electricity;
- Law of Income from Hydrocarbons;
- Law of Mexican Oil Fund for Stabilization and Development;[37]
- Regulatory Act of Article 27 of the Constitution in Nuclear Energy;[38]
- Mining Act;[39]
- Civil Liability for Nuclear Damages Act;[40]
- Law for Promotion and Development of Bioenergetics;[41]
- Law Declaring National Mining Reserves of Uranium, Torio and Other Substances from which Isotopes Hendibles are obtaining to produce Nuclear Energy.[42]

53. In addition, we need to consider the regulations passed under the new energy laws and a series of administrative rules issued by the regulatory agencies. Among others it is possible to mention the following:

- Regulation under the Act for Promotion and Development of Bioenergetics.[43]
- Regulation under Mining Act.[44]
- Regulation under Mining Act in the field of gas associated with resources of mineral carbon.[45]
- Regulation under the Act for Use of Renewable Energies and Supporting Energetic Transition.[46]
- Rules of the market (RM).

54. All these laws and regulations will be analysed in the following sections.

37. All these laws were published into the Official Journal of the Federation on 11 Aug. 2014.
38. Official Journal of the Federation 4 Feb. 1985.
39. Official Journal of the Federation 26 Jun. 1992.
40. Official Journal of the Federation 31 Dec. 1974.
41. Official Journal of the Federation 1 Feb. 2008.
42. Official Journal of the Federation 26 Jan. 1950.
43. Official Journal of the Federation 18 Jun. 2009.
44. Official Journal of the Federation 15 Feb. 1999.
45. Official Journal of the Federation 16 Dec. 2008 as amended in 2011.
46. Official Journal of the Federation 2 Sep. 2009.

§5. Role of Government Institutions in the Shaping and Administration of Energy Law and Policy

55. As mentioned, it belongs to the State leading the national development to guarantee that it is integral and sustainable. The State performs this role of direction through a number of ministries and a series of semi-autonomous agencies that define from various perspectives the energy policy, regulate energy sector activities and enforce energy and environmental laws in the energy sector. Ministries involved in regulating energy sector activities are the ME, the Ministry of Economy and the Ministry of Environment (SEMARNAT in Spanish). Among the regulatory and enforcing agencies are Regulatory Commission of Energy (RCE), National Commission of Hydrocarbons (NCH), Attorney General for Environmental Protection (AGEP) (Environmental Prosecutor), National Waters Commission (NWC) and National Agency of Industrial Security and Environmental Protection for Energy Sector (NAISEPES).

56. In fact, the Mexican energy sector is ruled from three different perspectives. First, from the strictly energy perspective; second, from the environmental perspective; and finally, from the economic perspective.

57. From the energy perspective, Mexican energy sector is governed by:

(a) the ME and its semi-autonomous offices;
(b) those autonomous offices (organisms) coordinated by the ME; and
(c) those coordinated regulatory agencies created by the constitutional reform of 2013.

58. From the environmental perspective, energy sector is under the supervision of the Ministry of Environment and Natural Resources and its three semi-autonomous bodies: NWC, Environmental Prosecutor and NAISEPES.

59. Finally, the Ministry of the Economy rules energy sector from the economic perspective. The following sections discuss on this regard.

I. The Ministry of Energy

60. The ME was established by a reform to the Organic Act of the Federal Public Administration passed by the Federal Congress in 1994.[47] In accordance with Article 33 of the mentioned Act, besides the general mandate of leading the National Energy Policy, the ME has the following specific powers:

(1) In regard to hydrocarbons industry: (a) to grant and revoke those assignments mentioned by Article 27 of the Constitution; (b) to establish those technical

47. *See* Official Journal of the Federation 28 Dec. 1994.

guidelines governing bidding processes, technical design of contracts; (c) to establish those areas to be the object of contract or assignment; (d) to allocate assignments and to grant permits for treatment, refining of oil, and natural gas processing (section VII).

(2) In regard to nuclear energy, to grant, deny, modify and revoke assignments and contracts for exploration and extraction of radioactive minerals (section IX).

(3) In regard to electricity industry, to review and, in its case, to authorize the Operational Rules of the Market (ORM) and to issue those administrative regulations of general character that make possible their supervision (section XXVI).

A. *The ME's Semi-autonomous Offices*

61. There are two ME's semi-autonomous offices: The National Commission of Nuclear Safety and Safeguards and the National Commission for Efficient Use of Energy.

1. National Commission for Nuclear Safety and Safeguards

62. The National Commission for Nuclear Safety and Safeguards was established by the Regulatory Act of Article 27 of the Constitution in Nuclear Matters of 1979,[48] as the responsible body for regulation and verification of safety of nuclear and radioactive installations, as well as safeguards, through the national system for control and accountability of special nuclear materials as well as regulation and surveillance of physical security of nuclear installations. The new Regulatory Act of Article 27 of the Constitution in Nuclear Matters of 1985 confirms in Article 50 the role of the Commission as the promoter of pacific uses of nuclear energy.

2. National Commission for an Efficient Use of Energy

63. The National Commission for an Efficient Use of Energy (NCEUE) is a semi-autonomous entity of the ME that has the aim of promoting energy efficiency. It is also the technical office for sustainable use of energy. According to the Act for Sustainable Use of Energy of 2008, the NCEUE substituted the National Commission for Saving of Energy. In accordance with its Article 10, this Commission is also in charge of enforcing the Act for Sustainable Use of Energy by imposing administrative sanctions in cases of non-compliance. In 2015 the Energy Transition Law repealed the mentioned Act. According to Article 17 of the ETL, the NCEUE is a decentralized administrative body of the Ministry with technical and operational

48. The Regulatory Act of Art. 27 of the Constitution in Nuclear Matters of 1979 was repealed by the currently in force Act passed on 1985.

autonomy. Its purpose is to promote energy efficiency and to constitute itself as a technical body in the field of sustainable energy use.

B. The Autonomous Offices (Organisms) Coordinated by the ME

64. There are three autonomous offices (organisms) coordinated by the ME: the National Centre for Natural Gas Control, the National Centre for Energy Control and the National Institute of Nuclear Research.

65. The National Natural Gas Control Centre has the objective of guaranteeing continuity and security in providing services to contribute to the supply of natural gas in the national territory.

66. The National Centre for Energy Control has the mission of warranting energy security. It does not have any power of authority but it is an organ for management and operation. The National Centre for Energy Control has the operative control of the national electricity system; it operates the electricity wholesale market, warranties the open access to the national networks of transmission and distribution. It does not have authority powers.

67. Finally, The National Institute of Nuclear Research is, according to Articles 41 and 42 of the Regulatory Act of Article 27 of the Constitution in Nuclear Matters, a semi-autonomous organ of the Federal Government in charge of conducting research and development in the field of nuclear science and technology as well as of promoting pacific uses of nuclear energy and to promote progresses in this field.

C. Coordinated Regulatory Agencies Created by the Constitutional Reform of 2013

68. The constitutional energy reform re-established RCE and NCH as independent regulatory agencies of energy sector.

D. The Regulatory Commission of Energy

69. The RCE was created in 1993 by presidential decree published on 4 October 1993, and it became the regulatory body of the ME in 1995 when the RCE law was published.

70. Later, the following Executive Decrees published in 2008 amplified the powers of this Commission:[49]

49. Official Journal of the Federation 28 Nov. 2008.

(1) Executive Decree that reform, add and repeal a number of provisions of the RCE Act.
(2) Executive Decree that reform and adds a number of provisions of the Regulatory Act of Article 27 (oil industry, basic petrochemistry and electricity generation are considered as strategic areas) the Field of Petroleum.

71. In addition, the Law for Use of Renewable Energies and Support to Energy Transition passed in 2008 provided RCE with new faculties and powers.

72. Finally, Article 28 of the Mexican Constitution as amended in 2013 ordered RCE to transform into a coordinated regulatory agency and Transitory Article 12 of the reform mandates the Congress to pass the necessary adjustments to the legal framework for the RCE, become coordinated regulatory agencies with own legal personality, technical and managerial autonomy; and to empower it to use the income from contributions and services that the law provides for their services in the issuance and administration of permits, authorizations, assignments and contracts.

73. In 2014, the Federal Congress passed the Law of Coordinated Regulatory Agencies in Energy Matters (LCRAEM).[50] The new law repealed the Law on Energy Regulatory Commission, granting RCE with its own legal personality and with technical, operational and administrative autonomy. Therefore, RCE is nowadays a coordinated regulatory agency of the Federal Government that directly reports to the Executive. Apart from those faculties and powers granted by the Hydrocarbons Law (HL) and by the Electricity Industry Law (EIL), Article 41 of the new LCRAEM provides RCE with powers to regulate and promote efficient conduction of the following activities:

(1) Transport, storage, distribution, compression, liquefaction and regasification, and the dispensing to the public of oil, natural gas, liquefied petroleum gas, petroleum products and petrochemicals.
(2) Pipeline transportation, storage, distribution and sale to the public of bioenergy.
(3) Electricity generation, transmission utilities and electricity distribution, transmission and distribution that is not a part of the public service and marketing of electricity.

74. To date, RCE is the agency that regulates all liberalized activities in hydrocarbons and electricity. The constitutional energy reform, the EIL, and the HL grant RCE the power to regulate all those liberalized activities in the energy sector, including electricity and hydrocarbons industries.

75. In the HL, the RCE's faculties are granted by the following Articles: 12, 17, 22, 46, 48, 53, 64, 70, 78 and 79. In the EIL, we can find the RCE faculties in the

50. Official Journal of the Federation 11 Aug. 2014.

following Articles: 12, 17, 22 and 66. Some of the faculties are: granting permissions to perform activities of transportation, warehousing, distribution, compression, liquefaction, marketing and sale to the public hydrocarbons, oil and petrochemicals; granting permissions to generate electricity and to provide electricity supply; to provide CECs; to verify compliance with the requirements for CECs, among others.

E. The National Commission of Hydrocarbons

76. NCH was created by law in 2008[51] as a semi-autonomous agency of the ME and with the purpose of regulating and supervising the exploration and extraction of hydrocarbons. The law expressly excluded from the jurisdiction of the NCH the following areas of activity:

(1) Refining, storage, transport, distribution and first-hand sales of oil and products obtained from refining.
(2) Processing, storage, transportation and first-hand sales of gas.
(3) Everything about the gas associated with deposits of coal.
(4) Processing, storage, transport, distribution and first-hand sales of products derived from oil and gas that are likely to serve as basic industrial raw materials, which constitute basic petrochemicals.

77. In 2014, LCRAEM repealed the Law of the National Commission of Hydrocarbons. As in the case of the RCE, the new law modifies the legal nature of the NCH transforming it into a coordinated regulatory agency for hydrocarbons industry, with legal personality, technical, operational and management autonomy (Article 3). In addition to those faculties granted to NCH for HL and for EIL, Article 38 of LCRAEM grants NCH the following powers:

(1) to regulate and supervise the recognition and surface exploration, as well as exploration and extraction of hydrocarbons, including its collection from points of production and to their integration into the transport system and storage;
(2) to tender and sign contracts for exploration and production of hydrocarbons;
(3) to manage, from the technical perspective, assignments and contracts for the exploration and extraction of hydrocarbons; and
(4) to provide technical assistance to the ME.

78. Besides, the HL grants to NCH the following powers:

(1) To grant contracts for exploration and production of hydrocarbons (Articles 11 and 15).

51. Official Journal of the Federation 28 Nov. 2008.

(2) To authorize partnerships or associations that engaged contractors (Article 15).
(3) To rescind administrative contracts for exploration and extraction and recover the Contractual Area concerned (Article 20).
(4) To authorize drilling (Article 36).
(5) To authorize activities of reconnaissance and surface exploration aimed at investigating the possible existence of hydrocarbons (Article 37).
(6) To approve plans for exploration or for development of hydrocarbons extraction activities (Article 44).
(7) To sanction conduct referred to in Article 85, section II of the Act.

79. Specifically concerning assignments, Article 7 of the HL vested the NCH with the following powers:

(1) to provide technical support to the ME in the selection of Assignment Areas;
(2) to technically manage and monitor compliance with the terms and conditions of assignments; and
(3) to approve plans for exploration and development for extraction and amendments thereto.

80. Regarding contracts for exploration and exploitation of hydrocarbons, Article 31 of the HL vested in the NCH the following powers:

(1) To provide technical assistance to the ME in selecting the Contract Areas.
(2) To propose to the ME's five-year bidding plan of Contractual Areas.
(3) To issue bases regulating the process of bidding and awarding of contracts for exploration and extraction.
(4) To conduct biddings for award of contracts for exploration and extraction.
(5) To subscribe contracts for exploration and extraction.
(6) To technically manage and monitor contracts for exploration and extraction.
(7) To approve, if any, modification, cancellation or termination of the Contract for Exploration and Extraction, pursuant to clauses shall be provided in the indenture and in accordance with the technical guidelines and economic conditions relating to fiscal terms that indeed establish the Energy Secretariat and the Secretariat of Finance and Public, respectively credit.
(8) To approve exploration plans or development for extraction, to maximize the productivity of contract area in time, and amendments thereto and monitor compliance with them, according to the regulation issued thereon.
(9) To provide technical support to the Secretariat of Finance and Public Credit and the Mexican Petroleum Fund for Stabilization and Development in the exercise of its functions in terms of the Revenue Act of Hydrocarbons.
(10) To approve, if appropriate, the annual investment programmes and operation of the Contract for Exploration and Extraction.
(11) To approve the transfer of corporate control or operations, in terms of the provisions of Article 15 of this Act and the guidelines issued to that effect.
(12) Any others established by applicable laws are Contracts for Exploration and Extraction.

(13) In resume, NCH is the regulatory agency in charge of governing all those strategy areas of hydrocarbons industry reserved for the nation that may carry out by private corporations or Productive State Corporations through contracts or assignments.

II. The Ministry of Environment and Natural Resources

81. According to Article 32*bis* of the Organic Act of the Federal Public Administration, the Ministry of Environment is in charge of defining and conducting national policy in regard to natural resources, ecology, environmental sanitation, water, environmental regulation of urban development and fishing activity as well as of enforcing and stimulating – in coordination with other Federal, local and municipal authorities – compliance with environmental laws and regulations (paragraph V).

82. Regarding energy sector, the Ministry of Environment is in charge of:

(1) evaluating and approving the environmental impact of energy projects;
(2) authorizing the land-use change in forest lands;
(3) granting concessions and allocations for national waters use and discharge permits; and
(4) issuing an additional number of permits, licences and authorizations that will be analysed in this monograph as well as to impose the administrative sanctions for violations of environmental laws and regulations and to file criminal and civil actions against violators through the Environmental Prosecutor, the NWC and NAISEPES. These enforcement agencies are semi-autonomous agencies under the coordination of the MENR. The next sections explain the role of each one of these offices.

83. These faculties are executed by the Ministry of the Environment through its semi-autonomous agencies: the AGEP; the NWC; and the NAISEPES. The next sections briefly explain the role of such agencies.

A. The Attorney General for Environmental Protection (Environmental Prosecutor)

84. The Environmental Prosecutor was created in 1992 as a semi-autonomous agency of the Ministry of Social Development,[52] whose jurisdiction was constrained to enforce environmental legislation in cases of sources of industrial pollution.[53] In 1994, the Environmental Prosecutor was relocated into the Ministry of

52. Official Journal of the Federation 29 Dec. 1982.
53. *See*: Reglamento Interior de la Secretaría de Desarrollo Social (Official Journal of the Federation 4 Jun. 1992) and Acuerdo que regula la organización y funcionamiento interno del INE y de la PROFEPA (Official Journal of the Federation 17 Jul. 1992).

Environment, Natural Resources and Fishing (MENRF), which later changed its name to Ministry of Environment and Natural Resources (MENR).

85. Currently, Environmental Prosecutor is responsible for monitoring compliance with environmental legislation, except as regards national waters whose supervision corresponds to the NWC. However, due to creation, the new NAISEPES, Environmental Prosecutor is not allowed to enforce environmental laws regarding hydrocarbons industry activities.

86. It should be mentioned that since its creation, Environmental Prosecutor has been a *sui generis* agency that holds powers of authority as well as prosecutor functions and even environmental certification faculties. At the beginning, it was said that it is not a real attorney in the sense that it did not represent the legal interests of society; however, the Wildlife Act of 2000 substantially transformed the role of Environmental Prosecutor in representing environmental interests, but only for the case of the application of the mentioned Act.

87. The amendments to the Federal Code of Civil Procedure in 2011 that introduced into the Mexican legal system collective action also strengthened the Environmental Prosecutor by conferring to it legal standing to file collective environmental actions (Article 585). The new Federal Law of Environmental Liability of 2012 stressed the trend to transform Environmental Prosecutor into a real Environmental Prosecutor.

B. The National Waters Commission (NWC)

88. An Executive Decree created the NWC in 1989 as a semi-autonomous agency of the Ministry of Agriculture and Water Resources.

89. According to the National Waters Act, NWC is a semi-autonomous administrative body of MENR (Article 3, section XII). In accordance with Article 9 of the same Act, NWC exercises the powers that correspond to the water authority and becomes a superior body with technical, regulatory and advisory nature of the Federation in conducting an integrated water resources management, including the management, regulation, control and protection of water public domain material.

90. The National Water Act (NWA) gives the NWC not only powers of administrative authority to manage national waters and their inherent assets and to grant concessions to individuals for use and exploitation thereof, but also powers of inspection and monitoring and indeed of collecting contributions (duties) for national waters use.

91. Article 9 of the NWA provides that for the exercise of its powers, the NWC operates: (a) through national central offices and (b) by administrative hydrological, regional level through its basin councils.

C. The National Agency of Industrial Security and Environmental Protection for Energy Sector

92. The NAISEPES was created by the Law of the National Agency of Industrial Security and Environmental Protection for Energy Sector passed in 2014[54] as a semi-autonomous agency of the MENR, with technical and administrative autonomy. According to the law, NAISEPES has the aim of protecting the people, the environment, and facilities of the hydrocarbons sector. As Environmental Prosecutor, NAISEPES is a *sui generis* agency. It is vested with regulatory powers as well as with enforcing and monitoring faculties. According to Article 5 of the law, the NAISEPES has the following powers:

(1) to provide technical elements on industrial safety, operational safety and environmental protection to the competent authorities for energy and environmental policies of the country and for formulating sectorial programmes in these areas. To do this, the agency will participate with the ME in developing the Strategic Sector Assessment;
(2) to participate with different levels of government, agencies and entities in designing and attending national and international plans to prevent and respond to emergency situations in the sector;
(3) to regulate, monitor and impose sanctions on industrial safety, operational safety and environmental protection in relation to the activities of the sector, including decommissioning and abandonment of facilities and integrated control of waste and air pollutant emissions;
(4) to regulate through guidelines, standards or other general necessary administrative provisions in matters of its competence and, where appropriate, through official Mexican standards, taking into account the opinion of MENR – in protecting the environment – and the Ministry of Economy, the NCH and RCE, on Industrial and Operational Safety;
(5) to define technical measures in the area of its competence, which should be included in the protocols to deal with emergencies or critical risk situations or situations that may cause serious harm to people or property and the environment, when the magnitude of the event is required and, if necessary, participate under the coordination of the competent authorities for implementation;
(6) issuing the bases and criteria for regulated subjects to adopt the best practices in regard to industrial safety, operational safety and environmental protection for the energy sector activities;
(7) to issue guidelines for the establishment and operation of management systems that should have been adopted by regulated subjects;
(8) to supervise and monitor compliance by the regulated subjects with statutes, regulations and other standards that is applicable to matters within its competence;

54. Official Journal of the Federation 11 Aug. 2014.

(9) to authorize public servants of the agency and accredit individuals or companies to carry out the activities of supervision, inspection and testing, evaluations and technical research as well as for certification and audits referred to in this Act;
(10) to file, conduct and resolve, in terms of laws and regulations, administrative procedures of its competence;
(11) to impose security measures or penalties that may apply under the applicable legislation;
(12) to decide on requests for revocation, modification and imposing fines, under the terms provided for in the applicable legal provisions;
(13) to establish mechanisms through which regulated subjects shall report incidents, accidents, emergencies, leaks and spills associated with the sector;
(14) to conduct research of root cause for incidents and operational, industrial and environmental accidents, according to the guidelines it issued to establish the bases for the regulated subjects to carry out such investigations, as well as the risk communication and lessons learned;
(15) to promote collaboration between regulated subjects in order to optimize the use of resources for the care of contingencies, emergencies, prevention and mitigation;
(16) to coordinate a certification programme on industrial safety, operational safety and environmental protection in relation to compliance with standards and performance standards, based on the principle of self-management and in accordance with the technical requirements established for such purpose;
(17) to authorize Regulated Management Systems;
(18) to issue, suspend, revoke or refuse licences, authorizations, permits and registrations in environmental matters, to which Article 7 of this law refers, in terms of regulatory provisions;
(19) to regulate and supervise in relation to matters within its competence, activities of capture, exploration, extraction, transportation and industrial injection of carbon dioxide, which are made to improve production of hydrocarbons;
(20) to regulate and supervise the production, transport, storage and industrial distribution of biofuels, as these activities are directly linked to the process of mixing or preparation of gasoline and/or diesel, in relation to matters within its competence, in coordination, where appropriate, with other competent authorities and according to the applicable regulations;
(21) to require regulated subjects information and documentation necessary for the exercise of its powers as well as the display of opinions, technical reports, test reports, contracts with third parties, studies, certificates or other documents of conformity assessment;
(22) to conduct studies of economic valuation of environmental externalities and risks associated to facilities, activities and operation of sector, based on a methodology that takes into account international best practices;
(23) to promote sustainable regional development and demand that activities related to the sector are performed, among others, subject to the protection, conservation, compensation and restoration of ecosystems, wildlife, environmental goods and services, in coordination with units competent administrative Secretariat;

(24) to provide technical support requested by the agencies of the Administration Federal Government, within its competence;
(25) to cooperate with the competent agencies, in monitoring mechanisms agreements and international conventions of its competence;
(26) to participate with the competent authorities in the design of the mechanisms of creation, administration, evaluation and accountability of funds that in its case are constituted to the attention of critical risks and major events;
(27) to propose its Rules of Procedure to president declared, through the Secretariat;
(28) to publish an annual report on its activities;
(29) to hire those consulting services, consulting, technical studies and research, required for its activities, and
(30) any other powers conferred by this Act and other applicable.

93. In addition to the mentioned agencies there are a series of administrative organs that also collaborate in managing energy sector. Next subsections analyses them.

III. The Ministry of Economy

94. The Ministry of Economy has the faculties of issuing the mining concessions, promoting the better use of mining resources and generating geological basic information. It executes these functions through the Mexican Geologic Service and the General Direction of Mines.

Part I. Regulatory Framework Concerning Electricity

Introduction

95. In Mexico, the first plants for electric power generation were built in 1879 and 1889. They were used by foreign textile and mining enterprises.[55] Later, Porfirio Díaz, who was President of Mexico from 1884 to 1910, granted the electric sector the character of a public service. At the same time, the first forty arc lamps were employed in Mexico City. This was followed by the illumination of the central boulevard with 100 lamps and later by the illumination of *Reforma Avenue* and other downtown streets in Mexico City.

96. Soon, the Mexican electric market attracted international companies with great experience and economic capacity. These included companies like the Canadian-based Mexican Light and Power Company that established itself in Mexico City and later extended to the centre of the country.[56]

97. The Mexican Revolution (1910–1921) emphasized that energy sector had a strategic and nationalist character. This was recognized in the Political Constitution of 1917 and later by secondary legislation. In 1918, a tax was established on oil lands and petroleum contracts to control the industry and to recover the resources alienated by Porfirio Díaz. That caused resistance from foreign companies. The battle to recover oil sovereignty ended when President Lázaro Cárdenas decreed the expropriation of the oil companies on 18 March 1938.[57]

98. At the same time, the Federal Government began to participate in the electricity industry. Faced with a monopoly of foreign companies, the government created, on 2 December 1933, the FCE. It entered into operation in 1937. Since that

55. In 1879, the first generating plant in the country was established at León, Guanajuato. This plant provided electricity for the textile factory *The American*. At the beginning this energy was used in production. In 1889, the first hydroelectric plant entered in operation in Batopilas, Chihuahua.
56. At the beginning of the twentieth century, private companies had an electrical generation capacity of 31 MW. In 1910 this capacity increased to 50 MW, 80% of which was generated by the Mexican Light and Power in the Necaxa hydroelectric plant (built 1900–1905) located in the State of Puebla. The Commission for the Development and Control of the Industry of Generation was also created as this time.
57. Tzibi M, *Ideología y praxis política de Lázaro Cárdenas*, 9th edn (1982) at 195.

time, the electricity industry has been considered a public service. Later the Federal Executive acquired the foreign companies, leaving them under the control of the FCE. In 1960, the electricity industry was nationalized following a reform of Article 27 of the Federal Constitution.[58]

99. From its nationalization in 1960, electricity has been managed exclusively by the State through the FCE and the Light and Power of the Centre Company (LPCC). However, in 1992, the Public Service of Electric Power Act was modified to open up opportunities for participation of private investment in electric power generation when it does not constitute a public service.[59] In 1993, the Act was reformed again allowing licences that had surpluses of energy of 20 MW or less to reach an agreement with the FCE or LPCC for its purchase.[60]

100. In 1997, the Regulation of the Public Service of Electric Energy Act[61] was modified to allow independent producers of energy to sell their production to the FCE.

101. In 2001, the Regulation of the Public Service of Electric Power Act was reformed,[62] allowing parties with permits for self-supply and cogeneration to alienate their surpluses with permission of the FCE or LPCC. However, this modification was declared unconstitutional by the Supreme Court of Justice, which held that the Executive Power had invaded the power of the Congress of the Union.[63]

102. The actions of the 1990s started discussion of reforming Articles 27 and 28 of the Constitution to allow the private sector, both national and foreign, to participate directly in the generation and distribution of electric power. In August 2002, the Executive Power sent to the Congress of the Union an initiative to reform the electric sector. That included: modifications to the Constitution, the Public Service of Electric Power Act, the Energy Regulatory Commission Act and the FCE Organic Act, as well as the creation of a National Centre of Energy Control (NCEC). The reforms are summarized below:

(1) *Reforms of Articles 27 and 28 of the Federal Constitution*: This initiative of reforms established specific rules:
  - the State is the only one authorized to provide the public service of electric power;
  - private investors may generate and sell electric power to the State or to the users whose consumption surpasses the minimum set down in the law; and
  - the State will guarantee access and non-discriminatory use of the transmission and distribution networks.

58. The nationalization of the electricity industry began with the purchase of the Mexican Light and Power Company and the American and Foreign Power Company.
59. Published on 23 Dec. 1992.
60. Published on 22 Dec. 1993 and entered into force on 1 Jan. 1994.
61. Published on 31 May 1993, reformed on 27 July 1997.
62. Published on 24 May 2001.
63. Published on 2 June 2002.

(2) *Reforms to Public Service of Electric Power Act*: The objective of this initiative is to provide the legal framework to authorize the participation of private investors in the electric industry. It also preserves the commitment of the State to guaranteeing the benefit of the public service of electric power. Among the main provisions are:
   - The FCE and LPCC continue serving the public service with electric power for all user requests without regard to the amount of consumption.
   - Users with consumption of more than 2,500 MWh per year in industrial, commercial activities or services will be able to opt for electric power supply through the public service or to obtain contracts with private generators.
   - Private investors may obtain permits to send electric power services to users that have obtained registration through bilateral contracts.
   - The Secretary of Energy is given the power to plan the National Electricity System, to dictate the necessary measures to guarantee the energy supply for the benefit of the public service, and to promote the use of renewable sources for electric power generation.
   - The Federal Executive will continue promoting the electrification of rural communities and supporting low-income energy users.
   - The NCEC will control the impartial use of the networks that integrate the National Electric System and will operate the generation system. The generation system will use the lowest cost plants to satisfy demand.

(3) *Reforms to the Regulatory Commission of Energy Act*: This initiative grants to the RCE jurisdiction to define the terms, conditions, and applicable rates for the following services:
   - the supply of electric power for public service;
   - the electricity conduction through the networks; and
   - the services provided by the NCEC.

(4) *Reforms to the FCE Organic Act*: The initiative of reform establishes the legal regime under which the FCE will operate. Among the main provisions are:
   - the *FCE* provides the public service of electric power;
   - the *FCE* is allowed to carry out additional activities to increase its revenues and to develop services of value to its clients;
   - the autonomy of the *FCE* administration must be considered by the Ministry of Finances and Ministry of Administrative Control (MAC) in the formulation of budgetary policy; and
   - the FCE will be administered by a Council of Administration and a General Director.

(5) *National Centre of Energy Act*: Through this initiative the NCE will be created as a decentralized organ of the Federal Public Administration. It defines the legal regime that will govern its functions:
   - It will enter into force on 1 June 2006 or when registered users acquire 12.5% of the generation of national electric power, whichever happens first. When that happens, the FCE will carry out the activities of this Act.
   - The functions of the NCE are detailed in connection with the operative control of the National Electricity System and the operation of the generation office.

103. As mentioned, by 2013, the state monopoly on the electricity industry was not absolute. Legal reforms passed in the 1990s had allowed private sectors to participate in generation of electricity that was not intended to meet a public service through various legal forms. Moreover, as independent producer, private enterprises authorized by the RCE were empowered to generate electricity to be sold exclusively to the FCE. However, as in the case of the oil sector, secondary legislation could not find full grip in the principles established by the Constitution on this matter. The constitutional reform of 2013 and the secondary legislation passed in 2014 formalized and complemented the process of opening of electricity industry that had begun in the 1990s.

104. This liberalization of the electricity industry entered a stage of regression from the start of a new government in 2018. In March 2021, the Federal Congress approved reforms[64] to the EIL that aims to return to the FCE the monopoly over all the activities of the productive chain sector..

105. The amendment introduced the following changes:

- Conditions the open and non-discriminatory access to the National Transmission Network and the General Distribution Networks to those cases in which 'it is technically feasible'.
- Introduces a new contract scheme called Electric Coverage Contract with Physical Delivery Commitment. Such a contract is characterized by including the purchase and sale of energy at a specific future time or date. Due to the intermittence of wind and solar technologies, a generator with this type of technology would be unable to enter into this type of contract.
- Modifies the economic dispatch criterion under which NCEC is governed, indicating that, in the dispatch criterion, physical energy contracts must be considered.
- Eliminates the obligation of suppliers to enter into contracts exclusively through auctions and establishes that they must enter into contracts with a commitment of physical delivery.
- Modifies the guidelines for delivering CECs, allowing clean plants built before 2014 to acquire them.
- Grants discretionary powers to the CRE to grant and revoke permits considering the planning criteria of the National Electric System established by the Ministry of Energy.
- Revokes the self-supply permits processed before the Energy Reform of 2013.
- Finally, it states that the contracts of independent electricity producers should be reviewed.

106. The reform to Electricity Industry Act passed in 2021 was challenged through three different legal resources:

---

64. The 2014 LIE has been reformed on three occasions, but while in two of them the changes are really minor, the reform published in the official journal of the federation on 9 Mar. . 2021 is transcendental.

(1) various *Amparo* trials;
(2) the action of unconstitutionality 64/2021; and
(3) two constitutional controversies.

107. On 8 April 2021, several senators filed an action of unconstitutionality before the Supreme Court of Justice of the Nation against the reform of the Electricity Industry Law.

108. The National Supreme Court of Justice analysed and voted on this matter in April 2022.

109. Given that only seven of eleven Ministers voted because the reform was contrary to the Constitution, obtaining the declaration of unconstitutionality was impossible.

110. The same year, the Federal Economic Competition Commission and the local government of the State of Colima filed before the SCJN constitutional controversies numbers 44/2021 and 45/2021 to combat the EIL reform of 2021. The SCJN resolved these legal actions on 18 and 19 April 2022. The SCJN dismisses both controversies considering that the actors did not have a simple legal interest to file them. Consequently, in these two cases, the SCJN did not decide on the constitutionality of the reform.

111. As a consequence of the previous, the 2021 Electricity Industry Act reform is still in force. However, several companies affected by it have filed *Amparo* lawsuits that sometimes suspended their effects. These trials continue their procedural course and will be resolved one by one in the sense that the judges decide, given the failure of the actions described above. Therefore, the constitutionality of the reform in question remains in doubt.

Chapter 1. Regulatory Framework

112. Currently, electricity sector is ruled by Articles 25, 27 and 28 of the Mexican Constitution, as amended in 2013, the EIL (2014 as amended in 2021), the ETL (2014), the Climate Change Law (2012), regulations of these laws issued by the Executive, and several administrative regulations issued by regulatory agencies. Among these administrative regulations, it is important to mention the *RM*. The RM governs the wholesale electricity market and is composed of two documents: The *Basis of Electricity Market* (BEM) and the *ORM*.[65]

113. The BEM is a regulatory body issued by the RCE that is composed of a series of administrative provisions of a general character aimed at establishing those principles that rule design and operation of the wholesale electricity market, whereas the ORM are those criteria, guides, guidelines, handbooks and procedures aiming at defining operative processes of the wholesale electricity market, issued by the NCEC.

114. As explained above, this new constitutional and legal regimen redefined monopolistic structure of energy sector. Articles 25, 27 and 28 of the Mexican Constitution (as amended in 2013) split the electricity supply chain into four distinct layers: generation, transmission, distribution and commercialization. In the same avenue, pursuant to Article 2 of the EIL (as amended in 2021), electricity industry comprises those activities of generation, transmission, distribution and commercialization of electricity power, planning and control of the National Electricity System and operational control of the wholesale electricity market.

115. The Constitution and the EIL clearly indicate that the unique activities of the electricity industry reserved to the State are (a) *planning and control of national electricity system,* and (b) *the public services of transmission and distribution of electricity.*

116. Under such constitutional basis, in 2014, the Federal Congress passed the new EIL. This law is regulatory of Articles 25, paragraph 4; 27, paragraph 6; and 28, paragraph 4 of the Constitution. The law is comprised of 151 provisions organized into 5 titles. Title I is composed of general character provisions, and it is divided into 2 chapters. Chapter I defines the objective and purpose of the law as well as a series of concepts whose meaning results important to well interpret the law. Chapter II establishes the powers and faculties of the different public regulatory agencies

117. On the one hand, Article 1 holds that the EIL has the objective of regulating:

---

65. In addition to establishing the procedures for conducting the wholesales transactions, the RM must establish the minimum requirements to be a market participant, determine the rights and obligations of market participants, define the way activities must be coordinated between transporters and distributors and define mechanisms for disputes resolution.

(1) planning and control of National Electricity System;
(2) public service of transmission and distribution of electricity; and
(3) other activities of electricity industry.

118. On the other hand, paragraph 2 of the mentioned provision indicates that the law has the purposes of promoting sustainable development of electricity industry and guaranteeing its continuous, efficient, and safe operation for the benefit of users, as well as compliance with duties of public and universal service of clean and low-emission energies.

119. Article 2 establishes the scope of the law by defining the following concepts:

(1) Electricity industry.
(2) Electricity sector.

120. The electricity industry is comprised of activities of generation, transmission, distribution and commercialization of electricity as well as the planning and control of National Electricity System, whereas electricity sector is comprised of the electricity industry and the supply of basic inputs for such industry.

121. In 2014 the Regulation under EIL was enacted establishing the administrative rules to enforce the law. According to its Article 1 the aim of the regulation is to establish those administrative provisions regulating planning and operational control of the National Electricity System, as well as generation, transmission, distribution and commercialization of electricity activities; to ensure compliance with obligations in regard to public service of electricity transmission and distribution and universal service that promotes continuous, efficient and safe operation of the electricity industry.

122. According to the new law, neither all activities of electricity industry are considered strategic areas nor the whole electricity sector has such character. In accordance with Article 2 the only strategic areas of electricity sector are:

(1) activities of transmission and distribution of electricity; and
(2) planning and control of National Electricity System.

123. By contrast, generation and commercialization of electricity as well as supply of basic inputs are not considered to have a strategic character.

124. Additionally, it should be noted that electricity supply is not specifically included within those activities regulated by Article 1 of EIL. That legal provision asserts:

> This law … has the aim of regulating, planning and control of the National Electricity System, the public service of Transmission and distribution of Electricity and any other activities of electricity industry.

125. Electricity supply could be included in the last part of Article 1 if we consider it as included in the idea of 'any other activities'. In this regard, Article 4 of the EIL states that electricity supply is a public service and therefore it is subject to the administrative law regime.

126. Title II refers to electric industry and it is comprised of eight chapters. Chapter I refers to planning and control of the National Electricity System. Chapter II governs generation of electricity activities. Chapter III regulates transmission and distribution of electricity activities. Chapter IV rules commercialization of electricity activities. Chapter V takes care of qualified users. Chapter VI regulates small electric systems. Chapter VII is about land use and occupancy. Finally, Chapter VIII deals with promotion of national industry.

127. Title III regulates the *wholesale electricity market* and it is comprised of just two chapters. Operation of the *wholesale electricity market* is the matter of Chapter I whereas Chapter II is about the National Centre for Electricity Control (NCEC).

128. Title IV is about participants in electric industry. This title is comprised of ten chapters: Chapter I, Duty of Public Universal Service; Chapter II, Social Impact and Sustainable Development; Chapter III, Obligation of Clean Energies; Chapter IV, Permits; Chapter V, Standardization; Chapter VI, Tariffs; Chapter VII, Investments of Productive State Corporations; Chapter VIII, Intervention; Chapter IX, Requisition; and Chapter X, Information.

129. Title V refers to infractions, and it is comprised of two chapters. Chapter I is about prevention and punishment of law violations and Chapter II refers to administrative sanctions.

Chapter 2. The FCE

130. As discussed above, under the constitutional reform of 2013, the FCE transformed into a *Productive State Corporation*. The new Law on the FCE was published in the Official Journal of the Federation on 11 August 2014. In accordance with Article 2 of the new law, FCE is a *Productive State Corporation* owned by the Federal Government that has legal personality and its own patrimony and enjoys technical, operational and administrative autonomy, as provided for in that Law.

131. According to Article 5 of the Law, FCE has the primary purpose of providing public service of transmission and distribution of electricity, on behalf of the Mexican State. In compliance with this function under Article 4, section I, the FCE shall guarantee open access to the National Transmission Network and to the General Distribution Networks when it is technically feasible, efficient operation of the electricity sector and free competition. Apart from that, FCE has the capacity, under the terms of that provision, of conducting distributed generation of electricity into units and commercialization of electricity.

132. Finally, in accordance with Article 6, FCE may carry out those activities, operations or services necessary for the fulfilment of its objectives. It can conduct such activities by itself or with support from its subsidiary productive corporations, or by holding contracts, agreements, alliances or partnerships with natural or collective persons from public, private or social sector.

133. In the same vein, within its public purpose, the FCE may conduct the following activities:

(1) generation divided into units and commercialization of electricity and related products, including import and export of these, according to the EIL and in terms of strict legal separation established by the ME;
(2) import, export, transport, storage, purchase and sale of natural gas, coal and other fuels;
(3) development and execution of engineering projects, research, geological and geophysical activities, supervision, service to others, as well as those related to the generation, transmission, distribution and sale of electricity and other activities that are part of its purpose;
(4) research, development and implementation of energy sources that allow it to fulfil its purpose in accordance with the applicable provisions;
(5) research and technological development required for activities it carries out in connection with the electricity industry, commercialization of technology products and services resulting from research and the training of highly specialized human resources;
(6) use and management of real state, industrial property and technology at its disposal to enable it to offer and provide any additional services such as, without limitation, construction, leasing, maintenance and telecommunications. The FCE will endorse and provide guarantees to third parties;

(7) the acquisition, ownership and participation in the ownership structure of companies with similar, analogous or compatible object with its own object; and
(8) other activities necessary for the proper performance of its object.

134. To achieve its purpose, the law provides that FCE may enter into contracts with individuals under schemes that generate higher productivity and profitability, including arrangements that allow them to associate and/or share costs, expenses, investments, risks and other aspects of the activities held by them, under the provisions to that effect issued by their Boards of Directors (Article 8).

135. Regarding the structure and organization of FCE, the previously mentioned law states that the Commission shall have the best-suited organization and corporate structure to meet its object, as determined by the Board of Directors. However, it is also important to note that in accordance with Article 57, FCE may meet its objectives by itself or through their subsidiaries or affiliates.

136. The law also defines in Articles 58 and 59 respectively what subsidiaries and affiliates are, as follows:

> Article 58. The subsidiaries productive corporations are productive state corporations with own legal personality and patrimony. They are organized and operated in accordance with provisions of this Act and provisions derived from it. Subsidiaries productive corporations will be subject to provisions of Articles 3, 7 and 8 of this Act and they shall cover the activities determined by the Board of Directors of the Federal Electricity Commission.
>
> Article 59. Subsidiaries of the Federal Commission of Electricity are those corporations in which it participates directly or indirectly with more than fifty percent of its capital, with independence of whether they are constituted in accordance with Mexican or foreign legislation.

Chapter 3. Electricity Generation

137. As per the Political Constitution of the United Mexican States, the generation of electricity by any source is an activity subject to free competition. In line with this constitutional principle, Article 4 of the EIL holds that generation of electricity is a service provided in a free competition regime.

138. The generation activity can be carried out by a generator with a permit or by a generator exempt from the obligation to have a permit. Generator is the holder of one or more permits to generate electricity in power plants, or the holder of a market participant contract that represents the mentioned power plants in the wholesale electricity market (Article 3, section XXIV).

139. In that regard, Article 17 of EIL points out that a permit granted by the RCE is required for generation of electricity only in two cases:

(1) when electricity is generated by power plants with a capacity equal or superior to 0.5 MW; or
(2) when electricity is generated by power plants represented by a generator into *the wholesale electricity market* without taking care of the size of the plant.

140. Exempt generator is the owner or possessor of one or more power plants that do not require or have permission to generate electricity in terms of this law (Article 3, section XXV).

141. The exempt generators basically carry out distributed generation. Distributed generation is the kind of generation that meets the following requirements:

(a) It is carried out by an exempted generator under the terms of this law.
(b) It is done in a power plant that is interconnected to a distribution circuit containing a high concentration of load centres,[66] under the terms of the *Rules of Market*.[67]

142. According to Article 68 of the EIL, distributed generation will have an open and non-discriminatory access to the General Distribution Networks, as well as access to markets where it can sell its production.

66. A loading centre, in accordance with s. VII of Art. 3 of the law, is composed with the installations and equipment which, at a specific location, allow an end user to receive electricity supply.
67. The *Rules of Market* are composed of two documents: the Bases of the Electricity Market, which establish the principles for the design and operation of the *wholesale electricity market* and its Operating Provisions.
See: Executive Order Issuing the basis of Electricity Market. Official Journal of the Federation 8 Sept. 2015 and Executive Agreement issuing the Handbook of the Market Information System. Official Journal of the Federation 4 July 2016.

143. In consequence, according to the mentioned Article 17, a permit is not required when two conditions are met: (1) a power plant does not have a capacity of generation equal or superior to 0.5 MW and (2) it does not operate in the *wholesale electricity market.* Generators operating under these two conditions are considered as *exempted generators.*

144. However, Article 16 of the Regulation under EIL states that, *exempted generators* may be required to obtain a permit from RCE when they will sell electricity in the *wholesale electricity market* without intermediation of a supplier. In this case, *exempted generators* change legal status and they become *non-exempt* generators. Apart from that case, Article 17 provides that without taking care of its generation capacity, power plants aimed exclusively to own uses in cases of interruptions of electricity supply or emergencies do not require permit for generation of electricity. In these two cases, according to section XXV of Article 3, owner or possessor of a power plant is considered as exempted generator as well.

145. A permit for electricity generation not only authorizes the generation of electricity but, according to Article 19 of the EIL, those who hold a permit can also carry out few commercialization activities, with the exemption of supply activities. This does not violate the principle of strict separation.

146. According to Article 3, section LII of EIL, the activities of supply that holders of a permit for generation cannot conduct are the following:

(a) representation of final users into the wholesale electricity market;
(b) purchase of electricity and associated products, as well as signing contracts;
(c) sale of electricity for delivery at load centres of final users, and conclusion of electric hedge contracts to satisfy consumption and demand; and
(d) billing, collecting and supporting final users.

147. In this regard, Article 18 of the mentioned law states:

> In relation to their own power plants production, generators are allowed to carry out those activities of commercialization mentioned by Article 45 of this law, with the exemption of supply providing. Over such activities neither the rules mentioned by Article 8 nor the strict legal separation are applicable to corresponding power plant.

Chapter 4. Transmission and Distribution of Electricity

§1. The State Monopoly of Electricity Transmission and Distribution

148. By the constitutional reform of 2013 transmission and distribution of electricity are activities reserved for the State. Under such constitutional rule, the EIL regulates this activity in Articles 26–44. According to Article 26, carriers are responsible for the National Networks of Transmission. The transmission and distribution of electricity are activities carried out by carriers and distributors, respectively. Carriers and distributors must operate their networks in accordance with NCEC'' instructions. NCEC will consider priority in the use of these networks for the dispatch of legacy power plants and legacy external plants with physical delivery commitment. Per EIL, carriers are those state productive corporations or organs, or their subsidiaries, that provide the public electricity power transmission service (Article 3, section LIV). Distributors are the productive state corporations or their subsidiaries that provide the public electric power distribution service (Article 3, section XXI). So, currently, the only state entity that has the category of carrier and distributor is FCE.

149. By EIL, private electricity generators only shall have free access to the transmission and distribution networks when technically feasible. Article 4, section I establishes that electricity transmission and distribution activities are governed, among others, by the principle of open access to the transmission network in non-unduly discriminatory terms.

150. On the other hand, the public service of transmission and distribution of electricity will be subject to those general administrative provisions issued by RCE in regard to quality, affordability, continuity, security and sustainability.

151. In addition, transmission and distribution are activities that have a public service character and so, its conduction is subject to *the general conditions for public services of transmission and distribution of electricity* issued by the RCE (Article 27).[68] Such general conditions have the objective of defining those rights and duties granting to providers and users of the service and include:

(1) applicable tariffs;
(2) characteristics, scope and modalities of the service;
(3) criteria, requirements and publicity of information to provide open and non-discriminatory access;
(4) credit conditions and suspension of services;
(5) scheme of penalties and compensations for non-compliance with contract commitments;

---

68. *See*: Ruling of Regulator Commission of Energy issuing general character administrative regulations disposition regarding open access to and provision of services in the National Network of Transmission and General Networks of Distribution. Official Journal of the Federation 6 Feb. 2016.

(6) conditions that, in its case, could be modified by agreement with specific users, under the condition it does not represent discriminatory practices and they are extensive to similar users; and
(7) procedure for transmitting complaints.

§2. The National Transmission Network

152. The National Transmission Network is composed of all electricity networks used to carry out electricity to the General Distribution Networks and the public and interconnections to foreign electrical systems determined by the ME (Article 3, section XXXV). Meanwhile, electricity networks are composed of lines, substations and equipment for transformation, compensation, protection switching, metering, monitoring, communication and operation systems, which allow the transmission and distribution of electricity (Article 3, section XXXIII). When those networks are used to distribute electricity to the public, in general, they are called distribution networks (Article 3, section XXXVI)

153. In accordance with Article 26 of the EIL, carriers and distributors are responsible for the National Network of Transmission and for General Distribution Networks. They will operate their networks according to NCEC's commands.

154. For maintenance of the National Transmission Network and General Distribution Networks that correspond to the wholesale electricity market, carriers and distributors shall be subject to coordination of and NCEC commands.

155. Carriers and distributors are obliged to interconnect their networks to those power plants whose representatives requested it and connect their networks to those load centres whose representatives request it under a non-discriminatory basis, where technically feasible (Article 33). A *load centre* is a concept that refers to facilities and equipment that, in a defined place, make it possible for a final user to receive electricity supply (Article 3, fraction VII).

§3. Carriers and Distributors of Electricity

156. As mentioned above, FCE oversees the state monopoly over transmission and distribution activities. Article 5 of the law of the FCE states 'the Federal Commission of Electricity aims to provide, in accordance with applicable law, the public service of transmission and distribution of electricity, on behalf of the Mexican State'.

157. Article 43 of the EIL's Regulation stipulates that carriers and distributors will provide the public service of transmission and distribution of electricity following the general administrative provisions issued by the RCE. These provisions shall contain, at least:

(1) The criteria for allowing interconnection and connection of users to the National Transmission Network infrastructure and the General Distribution Networks, taking into account the definition of general technical specifications, the specific characteristics of the required infrastructure and other relevant determinations in accordance with the law and the *Rules of Market.*
(2) The information that carriers and distributors shall make public, through electronic bulletins or other means of electronic access, regarding the capacity of their networks and the conditions of operation in the National Transmission Network and General Distribution Networks.

158. Carriers and distributors are governed by the open-access principle established in Articles 44 and 45 of the EIL's Regulation. These two precepts contain three rules:

(1) Carriers and distributors shall be subject to the regulations established by the RCE in relation to open access to the National Transmission Network and the General Distribution Networks, so as to guarantee effective access conditions, promote the development and efficient operation of the electricity industry and to avoid discrimination.
(2) In cases where carriers and distributors deny a user with available capacity and technical feasibility under the criteria approved and issued by the RCE, access to service or offer the service on discriminatory terms, the affected party may request intervention the ME and the RCE within the scope of their respective powers.
(3) Carriers and distributors shall be obliged to allow the interconnection of power plants and the connection of load centres to the National Transmission Network and General Distribution Networks in accordance with the general conditions approved and issued by the RCE and in terms of the *RM*.

159. Nevertheless, carriers and distributors are authorized to suspend connection or interconnection to the National Transmission Network and the General Distribution Networks for open access, in the following cases referred to in Article 46 of the regulation:

(a) Natural phenomena which have obstructed the execution of the works of connection or interconnection exclusively for the duration of the phenomenon and its effects.
(b) Social movements which prevent work from being done, only during the time when such movements restrict the carrying out of work.
(c) Other causes of overwhelming force preventing the execution of connection or interconnection work in the opinion of RCE.

160. In those cases, the RCE is empowered to initiate the investigative procedure to determine the causes of non-compliance with the open access obligation.

Chapter 5. Commercialization of Electricity

§1. Commercialization of Electricity as an Activity Open to Private Investment

161. Commercialization of electricity is not a strategic area reserved for the state. In accordance with Article 4 of the EIL, commercialization of electricity is a service provided on free-market basis. Under Article 45 of the EIL, commercialization includes supply of electricity and other activities. This provision states that commercialization includes one or more of the following activities:

(1) Provide electricity supply to end users.
(2) Representing exempt generators in the wholesale electricity market.
(3) Carry out the transactions referred to in Article 96 of this law, in the wholesale electricity market.
(4) Celebrate the contracts referred to in Article 97 of this law, with the generators, marketers and qualified users market participants.
(5) Acquire transmission and distribution services based on the regulated rates.
(6) Acquire and dispose of related services not included in the electricity market, with the NCEC intermediation.
(7) Others determined by the RCE.

162. Under Article 4 of the EIL, electricity supply is a service of public interest, so in accordance with Article 46, electricity supply requires a permission granted by RCE. That provision states in its first paragraph:

> Article 46. To provide the electricity supply or to represent exempt generators, a permit, in the modality of supplier, granted by RCE is required. RCE may establish specific requirements to offer basic supply and to offer last resource supply, and to promote efficiency and quality of these services.

163. The EIL Regulation reiterates this requirement in Article 18 by stating that permission granted by the RCE is required to provide the electricity supply service to final users, or to represent exempt generators in the wholesale electricity market.

164. Notwithstanding the foregoing, paragraph 2 of the quoted provision states that without prejudice of complying with measurement requirements laid down by the general conditions for the provision of the public service of transmission and distribution of electricity or by the MR, the following activities are not considered commercialization, so no permit or registration is required for:

(1) sales of electricity from a final user to a third party, when provided energy is used within the facilities of the final user; and
(2) sales of electricity from a third party to a final user, as long as the electricity is generated from distributed generation within the facilities of the final user.

165. The permit is not necessary when carrying on buying and selling operations that are not considered as commercialization by the EIL, such as:

(a) The sale of electricity made by an end user to a third party, provided that the electrical energy is used within the facilities of the end user, and
(b) The sale of electricity from a third party to an end user, provided that the electrical emergency is generated from distributed generation within the end user's facilities.

§2. Supply of Electricity

166. Section LII of Article 3 of the EIL defines supply as the set of products and required services to satisfy final users' demand and consumption of electricity, regulated by the RCE as appropriate, and that comprises:

(1) representation of final users at the wholesale electricity market;
(2) acquisition of electricity and associated products and signing contracts of electricity coverage, to meet such demand and consumption;
(3) sale of electricity for delivery at load centres of final users; and
(4) invoicing, billing and support to final users.

167. Supply of electricity is carried out by suppliers. Section XLV of Article 3 defines supplier as a trader holding a permit to provide electricity supply in the form of: (a) essential services provider,[69] (b) qualified service provider[70] or (c) supplier of last resource;[71] and may represent *exempt generators* in the wholesale electricity market. Sections XLIX, L, LI and LII of the mentioned provision distinguish among: (a) *essential supply,*[72] (b) *qualified supply*[73] and (c) *last resource supply.*[74]

69. Essential Service Provider is a Permittee that offers the Basic Supply to the Basic Supply Users and represents in the Wholesale Electricity Market the Exempt Generators upon request. Art. 3, s. XLVI of EIL.
70. Qualified Service Provider is a Permittee that offers the Qualified Supply to Qualified Users and can represent the Exempt Generators in a competition regime in the Wholesale Electricity Market. Art. 3, s. XLVII of EIL.
71. Last Resort Supplier is a Permittee offering the Last Resort Supply Appeal to Qualified Users and represents the Exempt Generators in the Wholesale Electricity Market that require it. Art. 3, s. XLVIII of EIL.
72. According to fraction XLIX of Art. 3, basic supply is the electricity supply provided to anyone – different from a qualifier user – that is requesting it under basis of a regulated rate.
73. According to fraction L of Art. 3 Qualified Supply is the Electric Supply that is provided on a competitive basis to Qualified Users.
74. According to fraction LI of Art. 3, Last Resort Supply in the Electricity Supply that is provided under maximum prices to Qualified Users, for a limited time, with the purpose of maintaining the Continuity of the Electricity Supply.

§3. Final Users

168. According to the EIL, the end user is the natural or legal person who acquires, for its own consumption or for consumption within its facilities, the electricity supply in its load centres, as a participant in the market or through a supplier. The EIL distinguishes between two types of end users of the electricity supply: qualified user and user of basic supply.

169. The end user is considered a qualified user when he has a registration granted by the RCE to acquire the electricity supply as a participant in the market or through a qualified service provider. In contrast, the end user is a basic supply user when he purchases this type of supply directly from the FCE.

§4. The Wholesale Electricity Market

170. The NCEC operates the wholesale electricity market (Articles 3, section XXVII, and 94 of the EIL). In this market, the participants may carry out those transactions indicated in Article 96 of this law. According to this provision, the wholesale electricity market comprises five sub-markets to commercialize electricity, CECs, power, related services and financial rights for transmission.

171. Following Article 94 of the EIL, only generators, wholesalers and qualified users can participate in the wholesale electricity market. The RM regulates its operation.

172. Article 96 of EIL also states that the RM shall establish those procedures that make it possible to conduct at least the following purchasing transactions:

(a) electricity;
(b) related services included in the wholesale electricity market;
(c) power or any other product that ensures sufficient resources to meet electricity demand;
(d) the above products through import or export;
(e) financial transmission rights;
(f) certificates of clean energy; and other products, receivables and penalties required for the efficient operation of the national grid.

173. EIL states that the wholesale electricity market is operated by the NCEC. This statement is held by section XXVII of Article 3 and Article 94. Article 95 repeats what was already pointed out by Article 94 in the sense that the 'wholesale electricity market will operate based on the physical characteristics of the national grid, and it is subject to provisions of *the Rules of the Market*'. In accordance with section XXXVIII of Article 3, the RM are: 'Both, the *rules of the electricity market* and the *operative provisions, governing the wholesale electricity market.*'

174. In this regard, Article 95 states that the RCE will issue *the basis of the electricity market* while NCEC will issue *the operative provisions of the market.* So, both authorities are involved in the approval of *the RM*. In terms of content, Article 96 states that *the RM* establish procedures that allow for at least transactions referred to in that provision.

175. Article 96 also notes that the *RM* shall establish minimum requirements for market participants; shall determine the rights and obligations of market participants; and shall define mechanisms for disputes resolution. Article 80 of the Regulation establishes that the *RM* shall at all times ensure a level and equal conditions for all participants in the wholesale electricity market and adds in twenty-three fractions the minimum aspects that these rules must contain.

176. By Article 98 of the EIL, generators, wholesalers and qualified users may participate in the wholesale electricity market after entering into a market participant contract with NCEC and presenting the corresponding guarantee in terms of the MR.

177. Generators, suppliers and qualified users participating in the market must notify the NCEC of each power plant and each load centre that they represent or intend to represent in the wholesale electricity market.

178. The general terms and conditions of the agreements and contracts that NCEC enters into with the market participants will be subject to the prior authorization of the RCE.

179. For the purposes of entering the wholesale electricity market, under Article 18 of the EIL, generators representing power plants interconnected to the national grid (those subject to permission from the RCE), shall:

(1) celebrate the correspondent interconnection contracts issued by the RCE;
(2) operate power plants in compliance with the instructions of the NCEC;
(3) carry out maintenance of its power plants in coordination and in compliance with the NCEC instructions; and
(4) notify to NCEC programmed withdrawals from their power plants.

§5. Tariffs, Prices and Compensations

180. In the wholesale electricity market, prices of transactions will be defined by the NCEC based on the received offers, under the terms of the *RM*.

181. Per Article 47 of the EIL Regulation, tariffs, prices, and compensations related to the public transmission and distribution service, as well as electricity supply in its modalities of basic supply and last resource supply, are subject to the exercise of the RCE's regulatory powers. In accordance with Article 48 of the EIL regulations, there are two types of tariffs: the maximum tariffs determined by the RCE and the conventional tariffs agreed between the participants of the wholesale electricity market.

§6. Emergency Supply

182. In accordance with Article 25 of the EIL, the generators and exempt generators are obliged to provide, to the extent of their physical possibilities, electric energy and related services when, due to emergency causes, the installations of the National Electricity System or the Electric Supply are or may be put at risk, fulfilling the instructions by NCEC only for such period as the emergency lasts. In these cases, exempt generators and generators shall be entitled to receive an economic compensation in accordance with the *RM*.

Chapter 6. Small Electricity Systems

183. Besides the National Electricity System, EIL regulates small electricity systems. In this regard, Article 65 states: 'Small electrical systems will be considered those not permanently connected to the National Transmission Grid and supply electricity to the public.'

184. As per Article 66 of the EIL, these electrical systems can generate and distribute electricity. The provision above states, 'When small electric systems have the authorization referred to in this article, the strict legal separation and the rules referred to in Article 8 of this ordinance shall not be applicable to them.' Finally, Article 67 provides that the *RM* may provide special schemes for the operation of small electricity systems.

Chapter 7. Import and Export of Electricity

185. The EIL does not explicitly refer to international trade of electricity. The EIL's Regulation states in Article 19 that generators and suppliers with a generation or supply permit granted by RCE and by registered non-supplier traders and qualified users may carry out import and export of electricity and other products referred to in Article 96. However, Articles 20, 21 and 27 of the Regulation suggest that these activities require authorization and that authorization shall be valid for up to thirty years.

Part II. Regulatory Framework Concerning Hydrocarbons, Gas, and Petrol

Introduction

186. The original text of Article 27 did not nationalize hydrocarbon resources. This article kept the principle of public dominion of hydrocarbons that was in force during the times Mexico was a colony of Spain but allowed participation of private parties in the exploitation of oil resources.[75] In that regard, paragraph 6 of Article 27 stated that nation's domain over hydrocarbon resources was inalienable and not subject to the statute of limitations.[76]

187. However, this article authorized the Federal Government to grant concessions for exploitation of such resources to individuals or corporations constituted in accordance with Mexican laws.[77] On such constitutional basis, the Federal Congress approved the first Petroleum Act in 1901. The objective of that law was to encourage oil activity through grating large concessions to foreign investors. The first concessions were given to 'Canfield and Doghein' and 'Weetman and Pearson'.[78]

188. In addition, Regulatory Act of Article 27 of the Constitution in the Field of Petroleum RA27CFP passed by the Federal Congress in 1925[79] recognized the

75. In 1910, President Francisco Madero introduced a tax of 3 cents per barrel of oil and a tax of 20 cents per tonne of petrol extracted by private companies.
76. According to Raúl Jimenez, Art. 27 of Mexican Constitution establishes the absolute property of the nation over hydrocarbons resources as well as the direct and exclusive exploitation of hydrocarbons by the nation: Jimenez R, 'Elementos historicos para la interpretación del régimen constitucional del petróleo de los mexicanos' in *El petroleo en la historia y la cultura de Mexico*, ed. Jose Alfonso Suarez (2008), 99–118.
77. According to Raúl Jimenez, Art. 27 of Mexican Constitution establishes the absolute property of the nation over hydrocarbons resources as well as the direct and exclusive exploitation of hydrocarbons by the nation: *See* Gersherson A, 'Hechos históricos importantes del petróleo en México', in *ibid.*, 57–61.
78. The history of petroleum in Mexico begins in 1900 with Mexican Petroleum if California, created by Edward L. Doghein, which began to drill on his property, named 'The Tulillo' in San Luis Potosí and discovered petroleum there one year later.
79. Official Journal of the Federation 25 Dec. 1925.

rights acquired by foreign petroleum companies on the basis of the non-retroactivity of the Constitution of 1917[80] and widely governed a regime of concessions that comprised the exploration, exploitation and transport of oil and hydrocarbons resources.[81] Confirming these criteria, by 1934, the Supreme Court of Justice recognized that Article 27 had no retroactive effect. In consequence, the Law of 1925 that established the procedure for private parties to request recognition of their acquired rights was absolutely constitutional, in accordance with the Supreme Court of Justice criteria.[82]

189. The first step towards the nationalization of the oil sector was not taken until 1938, when the Mexican government expropriated foreign oil companies' facilities. However, even after the expropriation, the nation's absolute property's constitutional principle did not govern the property of hydrocarbons resources into the subsoil in Mexico.

190. To nationalize this sector, it was necessary to introduce another principle into the Constitution: the principle of direct and exclusive exploitation of hydrocarbons by the nation.[83] Addressed to reach this objective, in 1940 a constitutional reform was passed to modify paragraph 6 of Article 27 in the following terms:[84]

> In the case of petroleum, and solid, liquid or gaseous hydrocarbons no concessions or contracts will be granted and the respective regulatory law shall determine the manner in which the nation shall carry out the exploitation of such products.

191. Since that time, the Mexican government assumed the monopoly of exploration, exploitation, refining and distribution of oil and other products derived from it.

192. One year before, the Federal Congress had passed a law in the field of petroleum to forbid concessions.[85] However, despite the constitutional reform, such law was repealed in 1941 by the Regulatory Law on petroleum that made possible

80. For some scholars the promulgation of such law was the result of the 'Bucarely Treaties' between the Mexican and United States governments. In such treaties, the United States of America recognized the governments that emerged from the Mexican revolution only on condition that the Mexican governments did not apply Art. 27 of the Constitution to the titles of property of petroleum companies issued by Porfirio Díaz.
81. *See* Arts 7, 8 and 9.
82. *See* 'El Aguila', *Compañía Mexicana de Petróleo v. Mexican Government* (1934) AR 88/28.
83. In his information to the Congress of 1938, President Cardenas stated: ' … to avoid as far as possible future problems to Mexico that estranged interests could cause it will be submitted as a matter of sovereignty that no concession of subsoil will be granted concerning petroleum and that the State has the absolute control of oil exploitation.' *See* J. Cárdenas, 'La irreformabilidad constitucional en materia de petróleo hidrocarburos', in *Exclusividad de la Nacion en Materia de Petroleo*, ed. J.A. Almazan (2008), 66–67.
84. Official Journal of the Federation 9 Nov. 1940.
85. Official Journal of the Federation 30 Dec. 1939.

the participation of private companies in oil industry through the so-called *contracts of risk*.[86] According to the Law of 1941, through *contracts of risk*, private companies could conduct exploration and exploitation activities and compensation for the services such companies provided could consist of a payment in cash or a percentage of the products obtained.[87]

193. Between 1949 and 1951, several *contracts of risk* were allocated to foreign oil companies.[88] Such contracts concerned hydrocarbon resources under a surface area of almost 4,000 km^2 of the Mexican territory. The payment to companies consisted of the total reimbursement of their expenses and investments, plus 50% of the value of the hydrocarbons produced by the perforated oil wells, in addition to compensation of between 15% and 18.5% of the production value over a period of twenty-five years.[89]

194. Given that such contracts were in contradiction with the constitutional principles as defined in 1940, in 1958 the Federal Congress passed a fourth RA27CFP. The new law created a legal system establishing absolute property in the nation over oil and hydrocarbon resources coupled with a public monopoly in the oil sector that included all activities related to the construction and operation of the infrastructure.

195. The Act of 1958 constituted an important step towards the configuration of a regime of absolute State dominion over hydrocarbons resources. This Act forbade for the second-time private participation in the oil industry. Article 2 stated: 'Only the nation may carry on the different exploitations that constitute the oil industry in the terms of the following Article.' Article 3 complemented that provision by stating that the oil industry comprises the exploration, exploitation, refining, transport, storage, distribution, and direct sales of petroleum products obtained from its refining; the exploration, exploitation, elaboration and direct sales of gas; as well as the transport and storage indispensable and necessary to interconnect their exploitation and elaboration.

196. A new step towards the nationalization of hydrocarbons was made in 1960 when Article 27 of the Mexican Constitution was modified again to introduce into its paragraph 6 the following text:[90]

> In the case of petroleum, and solid, liquid, or gaseous hydrocarbons, neither concessions nor contracts will be granted, nor may those that have been

86. Official Journal of the Federation 18 June 1941.
87. *See* M. Becerra, *Análisis constitucional de los aspectos más relevantes de la reforma energética* (2008), available at www.senado.gob.mx/reforma_energetica/content/foros/docs/20mayo2008_7.pdf.
88. In Bolivia, the Capitalization Act of 1996 introduced risk-sharing contracts for oil exploration and production.
89. The contracts were cancelled until 1970 by the Director General of PEMEX, Jesus Reyes Heroles.
90. Official Journal of the Federation 20 Jan. 1960.

> granted to continue, and the nation shall carry out the exploitation of these products, in accordance with the provisions indicated in the respective Regulatory Law. [Emphasis added]

197. The reform of 1960 also established that the absolute domain of the nation over subsoil resources includes the continental shelf, seabed, and subsoil of the submarine areas of the islands.[91]

198. Finally, to conclude the process of nationalization of oil industry, in 1982, Articles 25 and 28 of the Mexican Constitution were amended to establish that the oil industry is a strategic economic area and in consequence, is a monopoly of the Mexican State. In consequence, in regard to hydrocarbon resources, by 2008, the Mexican Constitution established a system of absolute State property with prohibition of concessions or contracts and a system of oil exploitation based on a State monopoly.

199. Notwithstanding the above, the Act of 1958 was modified several times to allow private investment in the oil sector. In May 1995, the Federal Congress passed modifications to the RA27CFP.[92] This reform allowed the private sector to build, operate and own systems of transport, storage and distribution of natural gas and other products derived from petroleum; in these cases, such products are not designated to be used as commodities for basic industries and in the specific case of gas for the basic petrochemistry.[93] As an adjunct to these modifications, the Executive approved the Regulation of Natural Gas. This regulation defines three types of activities subject to governmental permission: transport, storage and distribution. In the same year, a constitutional reform expressly excluded secondary petrochemical from the public monopoly of the oil industry.[94] In 1996, the RA27CFP was modified again to restrict further the areas where the transport, storage and distribution of gas and other products derived from petroleum can only be carried out by the State and to allow a wider participation of private parties in such activities.[95]

200. Eventually, in 2008, the law was modified to provide a legal basis for the public petroleum company, Petróleos Mexicanos (PEMEX), to contract multiple services and to enable private companies to participate in activities of exploration and exploitation.[96] Article 5 of the law (as amended in 2008) states: 'The Federal Executive, through the Ministry of Energy, shall grant exclusively to PEMEX and its subsidiary organisms the assignment of areas for oil exploration and exploitation.' However, Article 6 clarifies the meaning of the cited provision by stating:

---

91. This reform made it possible for PEMEX, the public monopoly currently in charge of oil exploitation, to have control of oil fields located in the Campeche Area.
92. Official Journal of the Federation 11 May 1995.
93. *See* Arts 3 and 4.
94. Official Journal of the Federation 2 Mar. 1995.
95. Official Journal of the Federation 13 Nov. 1996.
96. Official Journal of the Federation 28 Nov. 2008.

> Petroleos Mexicanos and its subsidiary organisms may contract with private parties and corporations, works and services required for the best realization of its activities. The payments established by such contracts shall be in cash and in no case shall the property of hydrocarbons may be transmitted to contractors for the works or services provided or for the works executed, nor can private parties and corporations be subscribed contracts for sharing production or contracts comprising percentages of production or the value of sales of hydrocarbons or their derivates.

201. Basically, the reform of 2008 reintroduced the contracts that had been prohibited by the constitutional reform of 1969 with the unique difference that, according to the new legal text, payments for such contracts should not consist of transmitting any property rights over hydrocarbon resources.

202. In consequence, by 2013, the State's monopoly on the oil industry was already relative. While the oil sector remained more into the governmental monopoly, private investment was already permitted in several gas industry activities. Moreover, the 2008 reform authorized PEMEX to contract with private individuals to develop those activities that the Constitution and laws reserve for the nation. Since that reform, *contracts of multiple services* were not regulated by the Law of Public Works and Related Services provisions but by the specific regime established by the PEMEX Law itself. Thus, secondary legislation that allowed the private initiative to participate in the hydrocarbons sector was subject to the constitutionality judgment.

203. The incorporation into RA27CFO (1958) in 1998 of the so-called *contracts of multiple services* was the avenue to avoid the obstacles established by the Constitution and its Regulatory Act for private investors to participate in energy sector as a whole.

204. The constitutional reform of 2013 and the Law of Hydrocarbons, passed in 2014, complement and formalize the process of opening the hydrocarbons industry that had started in the 1990s.

205. However, private investment has always been involved in the energy sector. In 2013, a constitutional reform gave greater certainty to private investors who already participated in the hydrocarbons industry.

206. This reform eliminated the absolute monopoly of the nation over all the activities of the chain of value. The reform just reserved to the government exploration and extraction of hydrocarbons. Under the new constitutional basis, in 2014, the Federal Congress passed the HL that rules both the activities reserved to the nation and the activities open to private investment.

207. However, in 2018, a new government assumed the Presidency of Mexico. The new government plans include neither opening the energy sector to private investment nor transiting to clean energies. Therefore, it has adopted a series of measures to strengthen PEMEX's position in the hydrocarbons industry. In that context, in 2021, the Federal Congress passed a reform to the HL. As analysed below, the reform aims to discourage private investment in non-strategy areas of the energy sector.[97] The amendment introduced two changes to the HL.

208. Following this amendment, the ME and the RCE can cancel granted permits in cases of imminent danger to national security, energy security or the national economy. But, again, the problem is that the reform uses vague concepts whose meaning is left to the authorities' interpretation, leaving private investors defenceless.

209. The second amendment eliminates the Asymmetric Regulation of first-hand sales of hydrocarbons and petrochemicals. Asymmetric Regulation in the energy sector refers to rules that aim to create a level playing field between private companies and PEMEX. According to this reform, the Energy Regulatory Commission (ERC) will no longer have the power to determine the price of hydrocarbons, petroleum products and petrochemicals offered by PEMEX in first-hand sales. Instead, PEMEX will set those prices, which places it in a dominant position in the market that affects free competition protected by the Constitution.

210. As in the case of the EIL, the reform to the LH also led to the filing of a series of *Amparo* proceedings by the affected parties. In some cases, a provisional suspension of the entry into force was granted and, in other cases, even a definitive suspension. However, some courts that have heard appeals against these suspensions have revoked them because the reform to the law is not self-applicable but instead requires a subsequent act of application, and it is at that moment when it could be challenged through an *Amparo* proceeding.

97. Official Journal of the Federation 4 Apr. 1995.

Chapter 1. Constitutional and Legal Framework

211. Hydrocarbons industry is ruled by Articles 25, paragraph 4; 27, paragraph 7; and 28, paragraph 4 of the Constitution; the HL of 2014 (as amended in 2021) and its regulations; the Law of PEMEX; the Law of the Mexican Petroleum Fund for Stabilization and Development; the Law of Revenue on Hydrocarbons; and the Law of Budget and Financial Responsibility.

212. The Political Constitution of the Mexican United States establishes the separation of the activities that integrate the value chain of the hydrocarbons industry by dividing them into *strategic* and *non-strategic* activities. Article 27 reserves for the nation activities of exploration and exploitation. These activities may be carried out either through allocations granted to productive state corporations or through contracts signed with foreign or national private companies.

213. The rest of the activities that integrate the hydrocarbons industry chain of value are considered non-strategic. Since these activities are not reserved for the nation by the Constitution, productive state corporations and private companies can conduct them by a permit granted by the ME or FCE.

214. The HL is comprised of 131 provisions organized into 4 titles. Title I sets up general character provisions and comprises Articles 1–5 that refer to property of hydrocarbons, the objectives of the law, the way the nation shall carry out exploration and exploitation of hydrocarbons, transboundary reservoirs and certain concepts that are relevant to well interpret the law.

215. Regarding property of hydrocarbons, Article 1 confirms the constitutional principle according to which 'it corresponds to the nation the direct, inalienable and imprescriptible property of all hydrocarbons placed into the subsoil of national territory, including continental shelf and exclusive economic zone placed out of territorial sea and adjacent to it'. The HL defines hydrocarbons as oil, natural gas, condensate, liquefied natural gas and methane hydrates (Article 4, fraction XX). So, provisions of this legal body govern both oil and gas. Additionally, the HL defines petrol as those products obtained from oil refining or gas processing such as gasoline, diesel, kerosene, fuel oil and LPG. These products are regulated by the HL in its Chapter 1 of Title III that refers to other activities of hydrocarbons industry, specifically this chapter requires obtaining a permit from RCE to conduct a series of activities related to these products. This issue will be discussed in the subsection of permits.

216. According to Article 2, the HL has the aim of regulating hydrocarbons industry. However, the concept 'hydrocarbons industry' is not so far from the concept 'oil industry' used by the Regulatory Act of Article 27 in the Field of Petroleum of 1958. In accordance with the new concept, hydrocarbons industry comprises the following activities:

(1) Identification and superficial exploration of hydrocarbons.

(2) Hydrocarbons exploration and extraction.
(3) Processing, refining, selling, commercialization, transport, and storage of oil.
(4) Processing, compressing, liquefaction, decompression and regasification, as well as transport, storage, distribution and sale of natural gas.
(5) Transport, storage, distribution and sale to public of oil liquefied gas.
(6) Transport, storage, distribution and sale to public of petroleum products.
(7) Transport by pipelines and storage linked to pipelines, of petrochemicals.

217. Concerning how the nation will carry out the exploration and exploitation of hydrocarbons, the new law provides that:

(1) In accordance with Articles 25, paragraph 4; 27, paragraph 7 and 28, paragraph 4 of the Political Constitution of the Mexican United States, the nation will carry out exploration and extraction of hydrocarbons (Article 3).
(2) Exploration and extraction of hydrocarbons mentioned in section I of Article 2 of this law are considered to have a strategic importance under the terms of paragraph 4 of Article 28 of the Constitution.
(3) The nation will exclusively carry out those activities mentioned in the preceding paragraph, through assignees and contractors.

218. Therefore, unlike what the 1958 Act established in this regard, according to the new HL, there is no longer a state monopoly on all activities that integrate the oil industry. Just activities of exploration and extraction of hydrocarbons are formally reserved to the nation because they are considered strategic areas by the Constitution. However, the new law does not prohibit participation of private investors in such activities since Article 5 states that the state monopoly on these activities shall be exercised through assignees and contractors.

219. It is relevant to mention that activities of reconnaissance and surface exploration are not considered as strategic and therefore neither are reserved to the nation nor are subjected to schemes of assignation or contract.

220. Moreover, the rest of the activities that in accordance with Article 2 of the HL comprising the hydrocarbons industry may be conducted by both PEMEX or any other Productive State Corporation or semi-governmental entities and individuals who have prior authorization or permission.

221. According to Article 1 of the new law, transboundary reservoirs are those sites placed within national jurisdiction that have physical continuity beyond it, as well as those sites or *reservoirs*, beyond national jurisdiction, shared with other countries in accordance with the treaties signed by Mexico or under the provisions of the United Nations Convention on Law of the Sea (UNCLOS).

222. However, Article 3 states in its paragraph 2 that exploration and extraction of hydrocarbons in transboundary reservoirs may be carried out under the terms of the treaties and agreements to which Mexico is a party. In this regard, it is important to mention that in 2012, Mexico and the United States of America signed the Treaty on transboundary reservoirs.

223. In the Gulf of Mexico, there are two hydrocarbon polygons (western and eastern) that did not appear either in the Mexican Economic Exclusive Zone or in those of the United States or Cuba. According to the International Law of the Sea, Mexico and the US could claim the entire Western Polygon whereas Cuba, Mexico and US could claim the entire Eastern Polygon.[98]

224. To avoid a potential conflict, talks began in 1998 to delimit the Western Polygon in the Gulf of Mexico. The existence of hydrocarbons in the Western Polygon in the Gulf of Mexico resulted, in 2000, during the Government of the Mexican President Ernesto Zedillo, in an agreement signed by Chancellor Rosario Green and US Secretary of State Madeleine Albright, to delimit the remaining area in the western Gulf of Mexico. However, before addressing a possible cross-border deposit, both parties chose to establish a ten-year moratorium 'so that none of the Parties, or their companies, will carry out [exploratory drilling] in the Polygon'. Mexico's preliminary offer was to establish a revocable moratorium only when the Parties reach an agreement on a specific area within of the Polygon.

225. In the case of the Eastern Polygon, on 18 January 2017, Mexico and Cuba signed a Treaty on the Delimitation of the Continental Shelf in the Eastern Polygon in the Gulf of Mexico, beyond 200 miles. Unlike the treaty concluded with the United States of America, this international instrument does not regulate the exploration and joint exploitation of the hydrocarbons in the Eastern Polygon. Rather, in accordance with its Article IV, 1, the parties commit, for a period of five years, not to authorize or allow drilling or exploitation of oil or natural gas in the continental shelf within a nautical mile, four decimal places on each side of the limit established in Article.

226. Finally, Article 4 defines a set of concepts that will be analysed just in those cases where it is necessary for the proper interpretation of the substantive law provisions in the following sections.

227. Title II of the HL refers to strategic activities of hydrocarbons industry, which are: exploration and extraction. This title includes Articles 6–47 and it is divided into five chapters. Chapter I regulates assignments. Chapter II rules contracts for the exploration and extraction of hydrocarbons. Chapter III regulates ownership of information obtained from reconnaissance and surface exploration, exploration and extraction of hydrocarbons. Chapter IV regulates the series of authorizations required to develop activities relating to oil and gas industry. Finally, Chapter V defines obligations of those developing strategic activities in the field of hydrocarbons.

---

98. It is estimated that there are 172 billion barrels of crude oil and 304 billion cubic feet of natural gas.

228. Title III of the Act regulates all activities of hydrocarbons industry that do not have the character of strategic areas and consists of Articles 48–84 organized into six chapters. Chapter I regulates necessary permits for exercising such activities. Chapter II refers to 'Systems of transportation by pipelines and Natural Gas, Proliferous and Petrochemicals Storage'. Chapter III governs the new 'National Centre for Control of Natural Gas' (NCCNG). Chapter IV refers to the so-called open access to networks of pipelines for the transport of hydrocarbons as well as storage systems. Chapter V regulates fuel sales to the public. Finally, Chapter VI establishes the obligations of those engaged themselves in the hydrocarbons industry activities not considered strategic.

229. Title IV of the HL in organized into 8 chapters. Chapter I deals with sanctions. Chapter II refers to transparency and corruption combat. Chapter III contains provisions on jurisdiction over hydrocarbons industry, public utility, and procedures. Chapter IV refers to use and occupation surface. Chapter V regulates the social impact of hydrocarbons industry. Chapter VI relates to social coverage and the development of national industry. Chapter VII deals with industrial security and environmental protection. Finally, Chapter VIII refers to compliance and enforcement of the law.

Chapter 2. PEMEX

230. As already mentioned, PEMEX was born as a public institution, which became a public enterprise in 1971. In 1992, PEMEX adopted a new structure. Four subsidiaries integrated this company. Later, the constitutional reform of 2013 transformed it into a Productive State Corporation.

231. Following Article 5 of the new Law of PEMEX, this Productive State Corporation aims to explore and extract oil and hydrocarbons solid, liquid, or gaseous, and their collection, sale, and commercialization. It can also conduct the following activities:

(1) refining, processing, transportation, storage, distribution, sale, export and import of petroleum hydrocarbons and products obtained from its refining or processing and its waste and supply of services related to such activities;
(2) gas processing and industrial and commercial activities of petrochemistry;
(3) development and execution of engineering projects, research, geological, geophysical and supervision activities, supply of services to third parties and all those activities related to exploration, mining and other activities that are part of its object, at market prices;
(4) research, development and implementation of energy sources different from those derived from hydrocarbons to enable it to fulfil its object as well as the generation and sale of electricity under the applicable provisions;
(5) research and technological development required for the activities performed in oil, petrochemical and chemical industries, commercialization of technology products and services resulting from research and the training of highly specialized human resources; these activities may do so directly, through the Mexican Petroleum Institute, or through any specialized third party;
(6) use and management of real estate, industrial property and available technology;
(7) commercialization of products of own manufacture through marketing networks as well as supply of services linked to its consumption or use;
(8) acquisition, possession and participation in the sharing structure of companies with similar, analogous or compatible object with its own object; and
(9) other activities necessary for the proper performance of its object.

232. On the contrary, the same law establishes that PEMEX may count on productive subsidiary companies and affiliated companies to fulfil its objective. Article 59 of the Law of PEMEX indicates the activities that each of these companies can carry out.

233. The new law allows PEMEX to perform all sorts of acts, agreements, contracts, subscribe credits and grant all kinds of guarantees to the Federal Government and with persons or entities to meet its goal (Article 7), which implies the involvement of the private sector in all those activities listed in Article 5.

234. Furthermore, the law provides that to get its aims PEMEX may have subsidiaries and affiliates. The activities that can be carried out by each of these companies are indicated in Article 59 of the Law of PEMEX, which states:

> Article 59. – PEMEX will act through subsidiary productive companies to carry out hydrocarbon exploration and extraction activities, without prejudice to Article 63 of this law.
>
> The other activities of PEMEX may be carried out directly, through affiliated companies, companies in which it participates in a minority manner, directly or indirectly, or through any association or alliance that is not contrary to the law.

235. The law also establishes the differences between subsidiary productive companies and affiliated companies in Articles 60 and 61 to indicate that the subsidiary productive companies are State productive companies, with legal personality and their own assets, which shall be organized and operate in accordance with the provisions of this law and the provisions deriving therefrom and shall be subject to the conduct, direction and coordination of PEMEX; PEMEX subsidiaries are those in which this productive estate corporation participates, directly or indirectly, with more than 50% of its capital stock, regardless of whether they are incorporated under Mexican or foreign law.

236. Article 61 expressly states that subsidiary enterprises are not parastatal entities and so they are governed by private law.

Chapter 3. Reconnaissance and Surface Exploration

237. The first link of the hydrocarbons industry chain of value is reconnaissance and exploration. The HL defines reconnaissance and surface exploration as:

> 'All those evaluation studies that rely solely on activities over the surface of the land or the sea to evaluate the possible existence of Hydrocarbons in a given area; within these activities, works for the acquisition, processing, reprocessing or interpreting information are included' (Article 4, Section XXXII).

238. According to Article 37 of the HL and Article 6 of its Regulation, reconnaissance and surface exploration need authorization granted by the NCH. However, it also states that those who already hold an assignment or have entered into a contract to carry out exploration or extraction activities do not require a permit but need to give notice to the NCH and to meet information requirements set up by the Commission. In contrast, Article 37 states that permit for reconnaissance and surface exploration activities confer rights neither for exploitation nor preferential rights concerning Assignments or Contracts for Exploration and Extraction.

239. Article 6 of the Regulation under HL states that, to obtain the authorization to conduct reconnaissance and surface exploration activities, the corresponding request must be submitted to the NCH, which must contain the following information:

(1) The general description of the project, which must include the purpose and scope of the project.
(2) The areas in which the field data collection is intended to be conducted.
(3) Description of data acquisition plan to be performed.
(4) Description of technology to be used for data acquisition.
(5) Technical risk analysis for the case of field data acquisition.
(6) The programme for delivery of processed, reprocessed field data and their interpretations, as the case may be.
(7) Other information requested by the Commission based on its regulation.

240. In accordance with Article 32 of the HL, it belongs to the nation's geological, geophysical, petrophysical, petrochemical information and, in general, all information obtained or will be obtained from activities of *reconnaissance and surface exploration* and *exploration and extraction*, conducted by PEMEX, other Productive State Corporation or by any other person. According to Article 33, this information includes:

(1) acquisition, processing, reprocessing and geological interpretation of seismic monitoring 2D, 3D and multi-3C;
(2) preprocessing, interpretation of seismic data and migration velocity model in time and in depth;

(3) magnetic, gravimetric, geoelectric and magneto telluric acquisition; and
(4) any other information, which is obtained by other means different from those previously listed.

241. The mentioned information will be administered by the NCH through the *National Centre of Hydrocarbons Information.*

Chapter 4. Exploration and Exploitation

242. The second and third stages of the hydrocarbons industry chain of value are exploration and exploitation, respectively. According to the constitutional reform of 2013, exploration and exploitation of hydrocarbons are the only two activities of the hydrocarbons industry considered strategic by the Constitution. Therefore, it reserves them for the nation. However, this does not mean a ban on private investment in those activities.

243. Title II of HL regulates both allocations to Productive State Corporations and contracts with private parties to conduct such activities. However, it is essential to clarify that, in terms of HL, although assignees and contractors are allowed to conduct these activities, they must also have the appropriate authorization granted by the NCH. Article 36 points out in this regard:

> Assignees and Contractors must have authorization from the National Hydrocarbons Commission, following the regulations and guidelines issued for such purpose by the said Commission, to carry out the drilling of wells in the following cases:
>
> I. Exploratory wells;
> II. Deep and ultra-deepwater wells, and
> III. Type wells used as design models.

§1. Authorization for Exploration and Exploitation

244. The HL does not describe the procedure for processing this authorization, but Article 36 states that such authorization shall comply with the time limitations under the Regulation issued by the NCH. According to this provision, if the Commission does not issue a response on the request within the specified period, it shall understand authorization has been granted.

245. Similarly, HL regulates causes for termination, expiration and revocation of approval.

246. Article 38 of the HL indicates that the authorization may expire by two causes:

(a) when exhibits any of the causes that are set up for the termination of permissions that Article 54 of this law refers; or
(b) when the contract for exploration and exploitation or the assignment has concluded.

247. Regarding the expiry of the authorization, Article 39 states that authorizations can be declared expired when holders:

(1) do not exercise rights granted by the authorization within 120 calendar days from the date of grant; unless previous authorization by the NCH, for justified cause; or
(2) incur in other causes of revocation provided in the respective authorization.

248. Finally, in accordance with Article 40, NCH may revoke the authorization if any of these assumptions occur:

(1) holder does not grant or maintain in force guarantees, insurance or any other financial instrument required under applicable regulations;
(2) holder does not comply with the regulation issued by the NCH and with the conditions set up by the authorization;
(3) holder does not pay applicable taxes and duties; or
(4) other causes established by authorization.

§2. Assignments

249. Articles 6 and 10 of the HL and 8 of its Regulation indicate that it corresponds to the Federal Government, through the ME, to grant, modify and revoke assignments for exploration and exploitation of hydrocarbons, prior favourable opinion of the NCH. Revoking assignments is only possible under the conditions established by Article 10. This provision states:

> Article 10.- The Federal Executive, through the Ministry of Energy, may revoke an Assignment and recover the Assignment Area when any of the following causes occurs graves:
>
> I. That, for more than one hundred and eighty calendar days continuously, the Assignee does not initiate or suspend the activities foreseen in the Exploration or development plan for the Extraction in the Assignment Area, without just cause or authorization from the Commission Nacional de Hydrocarbons in the terms established by the Assignment title;
> II. That the Assignee does not comply with the minimum work commitment, without just cause, under the terms and conditions of the Assignment granted;
> III. In the event of a severe accident caused by intent or fault of the Assignee, causing damage to facilities, fatality and loss of production;
> IV. That the Assignee on more than one occasion sends fraudulently or unjustified information or false or incomplete reports, or hide them, to the Secretaries of Energy, Finance and Public or Economic Credit, to the National Hydrocarbons Commission or the Agency, regarding production, costs or any other relevant aspect of the Assignment, or
> V. The other causes established in the title of Assignment.

250. Assignments can be granted to PEMEX or to any other Productive State Corporation. However, it is pertinent to note that according to Article 6 of HL, assignments only can be given by exception and therefore, such decision shall be appropriately funded and motivated by the ME. In this regard, paragraph 2 of Article 6 states:

> For granting an allocation, the Ministry of Energy shall justify that it is the most appropriate for the interest of the State in terms of production and guarantee hydrocarbons supply and that the possible assignee has the technical, financial and implementation capacity to extract hydrocarbons in an efficient and competitive way.

251. Article 9 of the HL's Regulations stipulates that for the purposes of Article 6 of the Law in the following cases it is possible to grant an assignment:

(a) It is a geological structure that is estimated to contain Prospective Resources greater than 2,000 million barrels of crude oil and that can be incorporated as a Reserve in an efficient manner with the own resources of a State productive company.
(b) It is a field in which the State productive company has superior technical, financial and execution capacities to extract Hydrocarbons in an efficient and competitive manner compared to the market average.
(c) When there is a specific area that presents the ideal characteristics to promote the development of a certain technique or technology to increase the incorporation of Reserves or the recovery factor.
(d) When a Contract for Exploration and Exploitation is administratively terminated and it is necessary to operate temporarily in the Contractual Area, while a new Assignment is awarded or a new Contract for Exploration and Exploitation is put out to bid; or
(e) Any other case in which the Ministry determines that the Allocation is the most adequate mechanism for the interest of the State in terms of production and guarantee of supply of hydrocarbons and considering the economic and social return of the Allocation.

252. Translated with www.DeepL.com/Translator (free version) the grounds referred to in Article 6 of the HL as a condition for the granting of assignments must refer to two issues:

(1) That this is the most appropriate mechanism for the State's interest in terms of production and security of supply.
(2) That the assignee has the technical, financial and operational capacity to extract hydrocarbons in an efficient and competitive manner (Article 9 of the Regulation).

I. The Authority Responsible for Issuing the Assignments

253. Although it is the power of the ME to grant assignments for exploration and exploitation of hydrocarbons, paragraph 3 of Article 6 of the HL requires the prior and favourable opinion of the NCH, which must be issued through a technical opinion. For this purpose, Article 10 of the Regulations states that the ministry shall send the proposal for an allocation area to the NCH so that the Commission may issue the corresponding technical report within twenty working days. In exercising this faculty, the Commission may request from the State Productive Corporation the information it considers necessary to issue such an opinion, which shall be forwarded to the Commission within fifteen working days.

254. According to Article 11 of the Regulation, the Commission's technical opinion must contain:

(a) The opinion of the Commission that will include, at least, the analysis on compliance with any of the cases contemplated in Article 6 of the Regulation.
(b) Where appropriate, the adjustment to the proposal for an allocation area submitted by the ME.

II. The Granting of Assignments

255. The HL does not deal with this issue, but Article 12 of its Regulations states that the ME shall decide on the granting of the assignment within fifteen working days following the receipt of the technical opinion issued by the Commission. The title of the allocation shall be issued in triplicate. One copy will be given to the NCH, another to the assignee and a certified copy is sent to the Ministry of Finances.

256. The ME shall also notify the Mexican Petroleum Fund regarding the subscription of the assignment title on a working day following such subscription.

257. As provided in Article 13 of the Regulations, the ME shall establish the following terms and conditions in the title of assignment:

(a) Description of exploration works and their periods, if any.
(b) Description of the exploitation works and their periods, if applicable.
(c) Other matters established by the ME.

258. In addition to the above, the assignment title should include the minimum percentage of national content to be determined by the ministry (Article 14 of the Regulation). Although the content of Article 14 of the Regulation is not explicit on this matter, it is understood that the ME has the power to determine the percentage of national content. However, to do so, it must hear the opinion of the Ministry of Economy. Article 14 of the Regulation indicates that the ME should consider that the percentage of national content does not generate unfair advantages that could affect the competitive position of assignees or contractors.

III. Correction, Surrender and Revocation of the Assignment

259. Revocation is a faculty that the ME may exercise without consulting the opinion of the NCH. Article 10 of the HL states that the Federal Executive, through the ME, may revoke an assignment and recover the assigned area when any of the following serious causes arise:

(1) Without justified cause or authorization from the NCH, for more than 180 calendar days on a continuous basis, the assignee does not initiate or suspend the activities contemplated in the exploration or development plan for extraction in the area of assignment for more than 180 calendar days on a continuous basis.
(2) The assignee does not fulfil the minimum work commitments, without justified cause, in accordance with terms and conditions of the granted assignment.
(3) The occurrence of a serious accident caused by intention or negligence of the assignee, resulting in damage to installations, fatality and loss of production.
(4) The assignee on more than one occasion intentionally or unjustifiably remits false or incomplete information or reports, or conceals them, to the Ministries of Energy and Finance, and to the NCH or to NAISEPES, regarding production, costs or any other relevant aspect of the assignment.
(5) Other causes established in the Title of Allocation.

260. The HL and its Regulation briefly regulate the revocation procedure. First, Article 22 of the Regulation states that the Ministries of Finance and Economy, the Mexican Petroleum Fund, the Commission or NAISEPES may submit for consideration of the ME at any time the existence of possible causes for revocation indicated in Article 10 of the HL. However, it is up to the ME to decide whether or not to initiate the revocation procedure. Article 25 authorizes the ME not to initiate this procedure when, in its opinion, there are cases of fortuitous circumstances, force majeure or other cases established by the title of the assignment.

261. Suppose the ME decides to initiate the revocation procedure, in that case, it shall previously notify the assignee of the existence of the causes invoked so that the assignee may, within a maximum period of thirty calendar days from the date of notification, state what is in his or her right to do and, where appropriate, provide such evidence as he or she considers relevant (Article 10, paragraph 2 of the HL).

262. According to such provision, if the assignee proves the cause for revocation is not admissible before the ME issues the respective resolution, the procedure initiated shall be terminated upon acceptance and verification by the ME. The authority will apply the corresponding penalties following the provisions of the HL.

263. In this case, it appears that the concession holder may exercise this right even after the expiration of the thirty calendar days that the law grants him/her for the exercise of the due procedure principle, under the condition that he/she does so before the corresponding resolution is issued.

264. Once the thirty calendar days period referred to in paragraph 2 of Article 10 of the HL has concluded, the ME must issue a resolution within ninety days. Likewise, in terms of the last paragraph of Article 23 of the Regulations, the ME shall notify the Ministry of Finance and the Mexican Petroleum Fund about the revocation of the assignment on a working day following the date on which the corresponding resolution has been issued. However, in principle, this notification should not take effect until such a decision has become definitive and the holder of the revoked assignment has exercised his or her right of appeal before the competent authority. Once the revocation has become definitive, this administrative act will have the following consequences:

(a) The assignee shall transfer to the State without charge, payment or indemnification and in good condition the allocation area.
(b) The corresponding settlement shall be made in terms of the applicable legal provisions, as well as those established in the assignment title.

265. However, the assignee who suffers the revocation shall retain ownership of assets and facilities that are not related or exclusive accessories of the recovered area.

266. Finally, it is necessary to mention that according to the last paragraph of Article 10 of the HL, revocation of the assignment does not exempt the assignee from the obligation to compensating for any damages that may be caused in terms of Article 24 of the Regulation, it also does not exempt the assignee from other legal administrative sanctions that may be applicable.

267. In addition to revocation, Article 8 of the HL also refers to transmission and renouncing rights protected by an assignment. Article 8 states that transmission requires previous authorization from the ME, whereas renouncement requires prior approval by the ME and notice to the NCH. Renunciation of the assignment results in the return to the State of the assigned area without charge, payment or indemnification.

268. The Regulation also refers to the transfer of rights incorporated into the allocation and its surrender and adds some rules concerning the modification of the corresponding title.

269. The Regulation refers to transfer of these rights in only two provisions. Article 18 states that the transfer procedure begins with an application for authorization, which must contain:

(a) the technical and economic justification;

(b) acceptance of the proposed Productive State Corporation as transferee.

270. From reading the above-mentioned precept, it follows that to decide on the requested transfer of rights, the ME must evaluate the technical, financial and execution capacities of the State Productive Corporation proposed as assignee.

271. According to the same provision, the ME must decide on the request for transfer within forty working days from the date of the request.

272. Once the transfer has been approved, the resolution shall be notified to the Productive State Corporation concerned and shall inform the NCH, the Ministry of Finance and the Mexican Petroleum Fund of the assignment transfer, on the day following the date on which it becomes effective.

273. Finally, Article 18 of the Regulations states that during the transfer process, the assignee and assignor must carry out all the necessary activities to maintain the operational continuity of the assignment area and to carry out the transfer in a well-ordered, safe and efficient manner.

274. Article 19 of the Regulation adds that the assignee productive state corporation shall be obliged to comply with the provisions of the assignment title and its annexes from the time when notification becomes definitive.

275. About the reassignment of rights incorporated into the assignment title, Regulation provides for three stages of this procedure.

276. First, Article 20 states that the request must be submitted to the ME and must contain at least the following information:

(a) technical and economic information of the allocation area;
(b) reasons for the resignation;
(c) a plan to ensure the continuous and well-ordered operation, secure and efficient transition of the allocation area in terms of provisions issued by the Commission.

277. Second, Article 20 states that the assignee must notify the NCH and the NAISEPES of the request for renunciation within five working days of its submission and must comply with the provisions established for this purpose in their respective areas of competence.

278. Finally, Article 21 provides that the ME shall approve the renunciation of the assignment when the following conditions are met:

(a) hydrocarbons security of supply is not affected;
(b) public energy policy is not affected;
(c) the Productive State Corporation has complied with its obligations and requirements in terms of the applicable legal provisions.

279. This decision must be issued within forty working days from the date the request was submitted. Issuing the resolution produces the following effects:

(a) In the event that the ME decides on the operational continuity of the allocation area, the renunciation does not exempt the resigning assignee from its obligations and responsibilities until a new assignment or contract for exploration and exploitation is granted.
(b) In the event that the ME determines the abandonment of the allocation area, the assignee shall carry out at its own expense and risk the plugging of wells, the cleaning, restoration and return of the allocation area to its natural state as determined by NAISEPES, as well as the dismantling and removal of machinery and equipment, in terms of these regulations, the title of allocation and other applicable legal provisions.
(c) The ME shall notify the Ministry of Finance and the Mexican Petroleum Fund of the renunciation of an assignment on a working day following the resignation is effective.

280. Finally, the Regulation also refers to the assignment title modifications in Articles 16 and 17. Assignment modification of the title occurs because of an authority's decision. Article 16 of the Regulation sets out the four cases in which it is possible to modify the title:

(1) change of terms and conditions, previous opinion delivered by the Commission within thirty working days;
(2) change of period of validity;
(3) any other case in which the ME determines that it is in the State's interest to produce and guarantee the supply of hydrocarbons and considering the economic and social return of the assignment;
(4) any other provisions as contained in the assignment title and its annexes.

281. Article 16 also states that the NCH may, at any time request the ME to modify the terms and conditions of the assignment title and that such request shall have the effect of the opinion referred to in section I of Article 16.

282. Because of this request, the ME shall notify the assignee on the beginning of the modification procedure, in accordance with the Federal Law of Administrative Procedure, within ten working days, the assignee may declare what is appropriate to his or her right, as well as to deliver the supporting documents and other elements considered appropriate.

283. Article 17 of the Regulation states that if, for the Commission's consideration, the modification of the assignment title affects the exploration plan or the development plan for exploitation, the assignee must submit the corresponding modified plan for approval, under the terms and in accordance with the procedure established by that authority in the regulation.

284. Finally, once the modification procedure has been completed, the ME shall notify the Commission, the Ministry of Finance and the Mexican Petroleum Fund of the modifications made to an assignment on the following working day that the modification came into effect.

§3. CONTRACTS FOR EXPLORATION AND EXPLOITATION

285. Coming into contracts for the execution of hydrocarbon exploration and exploitation activities is regulated in Articles 11–31 of the HL and 26–59 of its Regulations. In this regard, Article 22 of the HL provides:

> Contracts for Exploration and Exploitation shall be governed by the provisions of this Law and its Regulation. For the purposes of its enforcement, commercial law and ordinary law shall be supplementary applicable, and as far as they does not contradict this Law and its Regulations.

286. Therefore, as stated in the last paragraph of Article 23, procedures for adjudication of exploration and exploitation contracts shall be governed by the HL, the Public Works and Related Services Act, and the Acquisitions, Leases and Public Sector Services Act.

287. In the same way, it is important to mention that Article 21 of the HL expressly states that in case of disputes related to exploration and exploitation contracts, the NCH and the contractors will not be subject to foreign laws in any case. However, the same provision cited above allows such disputes to be submitted for resolution to alternative mechanisms including arbitration agreements in terms of the provisions of Title IV of the Fifth Book of the Commercial Code and the international treaties on arbitration and dispute settlement signed by Mexico. To this aim, the provision states that, where appropriate, the arbitration procedure shall be as follows:

(a) the applicable laws shall be the Mexican Federal laws;
(b) will be conducted in Spanish; and
(c) the decision shall be made in strict accordance with the law and shall be binding and final to both parties.

288. The fundamental principles governing these contracts are set out in Articles 11, 15 and 23 of the HL. According to these provisions, only the Federal Executive, on behalf of the Mexican State and through the NCH, may enter into contracts for the exploration and exploitation of hydrocarbons. Contractors will always be selected through public bidding process that will be carried out by the NCH. Contracts for exploration and exploitation of hydrocarbons may be concluded with PEMEX, other State Productive Corporations and other legal entities, either individually, in a consortium or in a joint venture.

I. The Contractual Categories

289. The HL refers to the different categories of contracts for exploration and exploitation of hydrocarbons mentioned in the text of the transitory articles of the constitutional reform. Article 18 states that contracts for exploration and exploitation of hydrocarbons may be for services, utility or shared production, or licence. As will be seen below, it is the Hydrocarbon Income Law that defines the characteristics of each of these contracting categories.

II. The Bidding Process

290. As mentioned, according to Article 23, the adjudication of the contracts will always be done through public bidding. The procedure for adjudication through public bidding is regulated very briefly in the HL. However, the provisions of the Law are complemented by what is established in Articles 33–45 of its Regulation and by the provisions of the guidelines and regulations issued for this purpose by the ME and the NCH, which according to Article 23 shall establish the acts and stages that make up this process. In this regard, on 28 November 2014, the NCH published Resolution NCH. 11.001/14 in the Official Journal of the Federation, issuing the administrative provisions on bidding contracts for exploration and exploitation of hydrocarbons.

291. In any case, the law establishes the following rules on this matter:

(a) The bidding process for adjudication of hydrocarbons exploration and exploitation contracts begins with the publication of corresponding calls for proposals in the Official Journal of the Federation.
(b) Those interested in submitting proposals must comply with the prequalification criteria regarding technical, financial, execution and experience elements, in the terms indicated by the guidelines established for this purpose by the ME.
(c) At least ninety calendar days must pass between the date of publication of the call for proposals in the Official Journal of the Federation and the date on which proposals are submitted.
(d) The adjudication mechanism may include, among others, an upstream auction, a top-down auction or an auction at the first price in a closed envelope, in which case the envelopes shall be presented and opened at the same public meeting.
(e) Tiebreaking criteria should be considered in the bidding processes and included in the corresponding bidding bases.
(f) In any case, bidding processes shall be conducted under the principles of transparency, maximum publicity, equality, competitiveness and simplicity.
(g) Proposals may be submitted and analysed by electronic means, under the terms established in the regulation.
(h) The decision shall be published in the Official Journal of the Federation.

292. In general, Article 24 of HL states that the bases of the bidding procedure and adjudication of contracts for exploration and exploitation, which are made available to interested parties, shall:

(1) comply with the technical guidelines and economic conditions relating to the fiscal terms established for each case by the ME and the Ministry of Finance, respectively;
(2) indicate, among other aspects, the type of contract, the criteria and deadlines for the prequalification process and clarification of the bases, the adjudication variables, the mechanism for determining the winner and, if applicable, the modification of its terms and conditions; and
(3) have a prior opinion of the Federal Economic Competition Commission, which will deal exclusively with the prequalification criteria and the adjudication mechanism referred to in Article 23 of the Regulation. The opinion of the Federal Economic Competition Commission shall be provided within a period of no more than thirty days following the corresponding request; if the opinion is not issued, within the established period, it shall be understood as favourable.

293. According to Article 26 of the HL, cannot participate in the bidding process are those who:

(1) are disqualified or prevented by the competent authority from contracting with Federal authorities, in terms of the applicable provisions;
(2) have serious and unresolved breaches of previously awarded exploration and exploitation contracts;
(3) use third parties to avoid the provisions of this article;
(4) present false or incomplete information; and
(5) are excluded by the bidding conditions.

294. Finally, in accordance with Article 25, against a resolution by which the winner is assigned or the bidding process so contracts for exploration and exploitation is declared void, only indirect injunction resource is admitted.

295. Regarding timing for calling for public biddings, Article 29 of the HL states that it is up to the Ministry, with the assistance of the NCH, not only to select the areas to be bid but also to approve and issue the five-year plan for bidding of contractual areas and to establish the Contracting Model that better suit to each area. Article 33 of the Regulations adds that the ministry, considering the contents of the five-year plan, shall notify the Ministry of Finance and the Commission of the intention to call a bidding process to adjudicate a Contractual Area.

296. Section IV of Article 29 of HL also states that it is up to the ME to plan and carry out the planning and development of events for the promotion and dissemination, at national and international levels, of the bidding rounds. These events must be public, in accordance with Article 34 of the Regulations, for which purpose the ME must publish information on the areas to be bid and implement all types of mechanisms that allow feedback from interested parties.

297. Based on the few provisions contained in the HL regarding the bidding process, the regulation complements the rules of the stages that comprise it. Thus, we can say that the Regulation under the HL deals with the following three aspects:

(1) based on the five-year plan, the ME must notify the Ministry of Finance of the intention to convene a bidding process (Article 33);
(2) to issue the call for proposals, the ME must provide the NCH with the following information:
  - Identification of the contractual area to be bidden.
  - Technical terms and conditions.
  - Technical guidelines.
  - The economic conditions relating to the fiscal terms of the Exploitation and Exploitation Contracts, as well as those that must be observed in the bidding process, established by the Ministry of Finance in accordance with the Hydrocarbons Revenue Law and its regulations.
(3) the opinion issued by the Federal Commission on Economic Competition in terms of section III of Article 24 of the HL.

III. Cases of Direct Adjudication to Mining Concessionaires

298. The principle according to which a mining concession does not grant rights for the exploitation and exploitation of hydrocarbons does not apply in the case of natural gas produced and contained in the coal vein that is being extracted.

299. In this way, in terms of Article 27 of the HL, a bidding process will not be required and the contract for exploration and exploitation may be awarded directly to the holders of mining concessions, exclusively for the exploration and exploitation of natural gas contained in and produced by the coal vein. Therefore, this exemption does not apply in the case of natural gas present in the area corresponding to a mining concession but not associated with coal and in these cases, it is necessary to obtain the adjudication of the corresponding contract through the bidding process.

300. For each mine in which coal extraction activities are or will be undertaken, the request for the award of the Exploration and Exploitation Contract may be made. To this end, the applicant must provide proof to the ME, with the NCH's favourable technical opinion, that it has the economic solvency and technical, administrative and financial capacity necessary to carry out the activities of exploration for and extraction of natural gas produced and contained in the coal vein.

301. In this regard, Article 51 of the Regulation states that the licensee of a mining concession who is interested in obtaining the direct adjudication of a contract for the exploration and exploitation of natural gas associated with its coal mine must submit the corresponding application to the ME. In accordance with the above-mentioned provision, the application must contain the following information:

(1) the current mining concession title;
(2) studies that determined the existence of natural gas resources contained in the coal vein and the proposed Exploration and Development Plan for the Exploitation of these resources;
(3) the verification report referred to in Article 28 of the Mining Act. In the case of mining concessionaires who are going to carry out coal extraction activities, they shall submit documentation to prove that:
   (a) they have agreed on the complete financing of the project;
   (b) they have committed the purchase of major equipment; or
   (c) at least 30% of the total investment is required in the project for the acquisition of fixed assets.
(4) documents accrediting that it has the economic solvency and technical, administrative and financial capacity necessary to carry out the activities of exploration and exploitation of natural gas produced and contained in the coal vein;
(5) The document by means of which the Ministry of Economy informs the ME about the compliance of the concessionaire with the obligations corresponding to the mining concession title in case, including the obligations established in the Federal Law of Rights, as well as the proof of not having preventive records in the books of the Mining Public Registry by a jurisdictional authority that limit the rights of the concessionaire;
(6) The pricing scenarios used, the geological characteristics of the mining concession area, information on the quality of the Natural Gas contained in the coal seam, a description of the existing infrastructure in and around the mining concession; and
(7) other matters to be determined by the ME through administrative arrangements.

302. Processing this request consists of three stages which are briefly ruled in Article 52 of the Regulation as follows:

(1) within five working days from the request was filled, it shall forward to NCH for the emission of its technical opinion on the appropriateness of awarding the respective exploration and exploitation contract;
(2) the Commission will have a period of fifteen working days from the day the request was received to send the technical opinion to the ME;
(3) the ME shall notify to mining concessionaire of the decision in regard to its request within five working days from the receipt of the technical opinion issued by the Commission and, if favourable, on the initiation of the process to define the Model Contract, the Technical Terms and Conditions and the Economic Conditions Relating to the Fiscal Terms, in accordance with Article 53.

303. According to Article 53 of the Regulation, when a direct adjudication is granted, the following rules shall be applicable:

- The ME will send to the Ministry of Finance and to the NCH, within fifteen working days, the complete direct adjudication request, the resolution of the direct adjudication, the proposal of the Contracting Model that will correspond to the Contractual Area and the supporting information that is determined in the coordination agreements subscribed for such purpose by such agencies.
- Once the Contracting Model has been determined, the ME will have a period of twenty working days to define the technical terms and conditions and to request the Ministry of Finance to establish the economic conditions relating to fiscal terms in accordance with the Law of Revenue of Hydrocarbons and its regulations.
- Once the above stages have been concluded, the ME will send the necessary information to the Commission for signing the contract for the exploration and exploitation of natural gas associated with a coal mine, within five working days so as the NCH initiates its formalization.

IV. Conflicts Between Rights

304. If, after the bidding process carried out by the NCH to adjudicate a contract for exploration and exploitation of hydrocarbons, or if an allocation has been granted, and there is a possible affectation to a mining concession rights with respect to the surface area subject to the concession in which the extraction of minerals is actually being carried out, a period of ninety days shall be opened for the contractor or assignee and the miner's licensee to conduct negotiations and reach an agreement allowing the development of the project by the contractor or assignee.

305. Negotiation procedure and agreement referred to in the previous paragraph shall be carried out in a transparent manner and shall be subject to the provisions of the regulation and to the following bases:

(a) The contractor or assignee shall notify the NCH on the beginning of negotiations with the mining concessionaire.
(b) The compensation agreed upon shall be proportionate to the requirements of the contractor or assignee in accordance with the activities carried out under the contract or assignment.
(c) Compensation payments agreed may be paid in cash or, where appropriate, by the commitment to form part of the hydrocarbon extraction project, or a combination of both. Under no circumstances may a compensation be agreed upon for part of the hydrocarbons production of the project to be paid by the contractor.
(d) Compensation, as well as any other terms and conditions agreed between the contractor or assignee and the mining concessionaire, shall invariably be set forth in a written contract, containing at least the rights and obligations of the parties, as well as possible dispute settlement mechanisms.

306. In the event that the contractor or assignee and the mining concessionaire fail to reach an agreement within the ninety-day period referred to above, the NCH, with the assistance of the competent authorities, shall determine whether or not the two extractive activities can coexist and whether or not there is an effect on the rights of a mining concession in respect of the area subject to the concession in which the extraction is actually taking place.

307. In cases of no agreement and the NCH determines that there is an affectation on the rights of a mining concession with respect to the area subject to the concession in which the extraction of minerals is actually being carried out, the mentioned Commission shall determine the amount and terms in which the corresponding compensation shall be paid by the contractor or assignee, in favour of the mining concessionaire, in accordance with the respective valuation, or as the case may be, depending on the seriousness of the problem.

308. The NCH may authorize the holders of mining concessions to carry out specific surface exploration activities for hydrocarbons in the areas in which their rights coexist in accordance with the provisions of HL and the respective Regulation.

309. In the case that the mining concessionaires are carrying out exploration works and activities under their concession, they shall apply the provisions of this article in regard to the agreement with the contractor or assignee; if there is no agreement, the NCH shall determine the amount and terms of compensation in accordance with the respective valuation. For the provisions of this paragraph to be applicable in relation to the agreement with the contractor or assignee and, where applicable, the compensation, the works and exploration works of the mining concession must be included in the verification report referred to in Article 28 of the Mining Law, which was submitted a year prior to the publication by the ME of the areas that may be bid for hydrocarbon exploration and extraction. The verification report referred to above shall also be notified to the ME and the NCH.

310. The mining concessionaire that performs the exploration or exploitation of hydrocarbons referred to in Article 28, without having the corresponding exploration and exploitation contract, shall be punished in accordance with the provisions of HL and the Ministry of Economy, upon notice from the NCH, shall sanction such concessionaire with the cancellation of the respective mining concession in accordance with the provisions of the Mining Law.

V. The Content of Contracts

311. Article 11 of the HL states that the contracts for the exploration and extraction of hydrocarbons will invariably establish that the Hydrocarbons in the Subsoil are property of the Nation, but it is Article 19 details the aspects that they must deal with. The above-mentioned precept points out:

> Article 19. – Contracts for Exploration and Exploitation shall have at least clauses on:

I. Definition of the Contractual Area;
II. Exploration and development plans for Extraction, including the deadline for submission;
III. The minimum work and investment programme, where appropriate;
IV. The Contractor's obligations, including economic and fiscal terms;
V. The validity, as well as the conditions for its extension;
VI. The acquisition of guarantees and insurance;
VII. The existence of a system of external audits to supervise the effective recovery, if any, of costs incurred and other accounting involved in the operation of the contract;
VIII. Causes of termination, including early termination and administrative termination;
IX. The transparency obligations that allow access to information derived from the contracts, including disclosure of the consideration, contributions and payments provided for in the contract itself;
X. The minimum percentage of national content;
XI. The conditions and mechanisms for the reduction or return of the Contractual Area;
XII. Dispute resolution, including alternative means of conflict resolution;
XIII. Penalties applicable in the event of failure to fulfil contractual obligations;
XIV. The responsibility of the Contractor and the operator in accordance with international best practice. In the event of an accident, the Contractor or operator's liability shall not be limited if willful misconduct or fault is proven on their part, and
XV. The observance of international best practices for the operation in the Contractual Area.

VI. Contract's Expiration

312. Termination of contracts is a matter regulated by Article 20 of the HL. This provision indicates that Federal Executive, through the NCH, may terminate the contracts for Exploration and Exploitation and recover the Contractual Area only when any of the following serious causes arise:

(a) for more than 180 calendar days on a continuous basis, the contractor does not initiate or suspend the activities contemplated in the Exploration or Development Plan for Extraction in the Contractual Area, without justified cause or authorization from the National Hydrocarbons Commission;
(b) the contractor does not perform the minimum commitment of work, without just cause, in accordance with the terms and conditions of the Exploration and Exploitation Contract;
(c) the contractor partially or totally transfers the operation or the rights granted in the Exploration and Exploitation Contract, without prior authorization in terms of the provisions of Article 15 of this law;

(d) the occurrence of a serious accident caused by malice or negligence of the contractor, resulting in damage to facilities, fatality and loss of production;
(e) the contractor on more than one occasion intentionally or unjustifiably remits false or incomplete information or reports, or conceals them, to the Ministries of Energy, Finance and Public Credit or Economy, to the National Commission on Hydrocarbons or to the agency, regarding production, costs or any other relevant aspect of the contract;
(f) the contractor fails to observe a final ruling issued by Federal Courts, which constitutes a final determination; or
(g) the contractor omits, without justified cause, any payment to the State or delivery of hydrocarbons to it, in accordance with the terms and conditions stipulated in the Contract for Exploration and Extraction.

313. However, paragraph 2 of Article 20 adds that, without prejudice to these administrative causes, the respective contracts must establish other grounds for termination and rescission. The provision also regulates the termination procedure, which we can illustrate as follows.

314. First, the declaration of administrative termination requires NCH to notify the contractor in advance of the cause or causes invoked and shall be governed by this law and its regulations.

315. Upon notification of the cause of action, the contractor shall have a maximum of thirty calendar days from the date of the notification to state what is in its rightful interest and, where applicable, to provide such evidence as it considers appropriate. In this case, if the contractor resolves the cause of termination that it has incurred before the NCH issues the respective resolution, the initiated procedure shall be invalid, after prior acceptance and verification by the NCH and, if applicable, applying the corresponding penalties in accordance with the provisions of this law.

316. After the expiration of the thirty-day period following notification to contractor, the NCH shall have a period of ninety calendar days to decide considering the arguments and evidence that the contractor may have submitted.

317. In any case, in accordance with the above-mentioned provision, the decision whether to terminate the contract administratively shall be properly founded and motived and communicated to the contractor.

318. Because of the administrative termination, the contractor shall transfer to the State free of charge, payment or indemnification, the Contractual Area and the corresponding settlement shall be affected in terms of the applicable legal provisions and contractual provisions, to this end, the Contract for Exploration and Exploitation shall determine the terms of such transfer and the contractor's obligations.

319. Finally, the administrative termination does not relieve the contractor of the obligation to compensate any corresponding damages, in terms of the applicable legal provisions. In any event, the contractor shall retain ownership of property and facilities that are not related or exclusive accessories to the recovered area.

Chapter 5. Other Activities of Hydrocarbons Industry

320. All activities of the hydrocarbons industry not considered by the Mexican Constitution as strategic areas are open to private investment but subject to the authorization of the Mexican government through a system of permits and licenses that is fundamentally but not exclusively stated in Article 48 of the HL.

321. Article 2 of HL specifies those activities of the hydrocarbons industry not reserved for the nation. Among these activities, Article 2 includes sales of oil.

322. Article 48 of the HL states that the following activities are subject to obtaining a permit:

– Treatment and refining of petroleum.
– Processing of natural gas.
– Export and import of hydrocarbons and petroleum products.

323. According to Article 80 of the HL the ME grants these permits.

324. In contrast, it corresponds to the CRE giving licenses for:

(a) transportation, storage, distribution, compression, liquefaction, regasification, commercialization; and
(b) sale to the public of hydrocarbons, petroleum or petrochemicals as well as the management of integrated systems.

325. Article 48 does not require a permit to carry out activities related to selling oil. However, since the commercialization of oil is an activity that forms part of the hydrocarbons industry, according to Article 2 of the HL and not covered by Article 48, we have to conclude that this essential activity is not regulated. The Regulation of Title III under HL does not clarify anything in this respect. Although one can argue hydrocarbons include petroleum, it should be noted that Article 48 does not refer to first-hand sales of hydrocarbons.

326. Finally, Article 48 does not refer to the authorization to which, in terms of Articles 37 of the HL and 6 of its Regulation, recognition and surface exploration activities are subject.

327. The reform of 2021 to the HL significantly modified the legal regime of permits. One of the aspects that the reform to the HL modified is that according to the new text of Article 51, granting the permits to which we refer will be evaluated if the applicant has the storage capacity determined by the ME.

328. Another significant change is that Article 53 of the HL stated that the request is positive if the ME or the RCE did not resolve a permit request within the legal term before the reform. The reform modified this rule, and now the aforementioned lawful provision indicates that the silence of the authority has adverse effects

329. The amendment to Article 57 of the HL also introduces a relevant change. By the amended text of this provision, the authority that issued a permit may at any time carry out the temporary occupation, intervention or suspension of the license to guarantee the national interest.

330. In the same sense, the reform to the HL of 2021 adds a new Article 59 bis. The ME or the RCE may suspend the permits issued due to imminent danger to national security, energy security, or the national economy.

331. Finally, section XI of the amended Article 56 provides that the ME or the RCE may revoke the permits issued when, among other things, when carrying out activities of Transportation, Storage, Distribution or Sale to the Public of Hydrocarbons, Petroleum Products or Petrochemicals, which are proven to have been acquired from illegal way or for the commission of the crime of smuggling Hydrocarbons, Petroleum Products and Petrochemicals

Chapter 6. Transport and Storage of Hydrocarbons

332. The HL dedicates Chapter II of Title III to regulate Natural Gas, Oil and Petrochemicals Pipeline Transportation and Storage Systems. Article 60 of this law allows the natural gas pipeline transportation and storage systems that are interconnected to form integrated systems to expand coverage or provide systemic benefits in terms of improvements in safety, continuity, quality, and efficiency in delivering services.

333. Construction of integrated systems requires authorization granted by the RCE, but the ME may subject it to specific requirements through a public energy policy issuance. Integrated systems operation corresponds to a manager, a public, private, or public-private entity, and will require a specific permit issued by the RCE.

334. According to Article 62 of the HL, the managers oversee the following activities:

I. To coordinate the different Pipeline Transport and Storage Permit holders to achieve continuity, quality, safety, and efficiency in services provisioning, to guarantee adequate open access and not unduly discriminatory,
II. To be responsible for the payment obligations of tariffs of the Transport or Storage systems that integrate the Integrated System, in the terms determined by the Energy Regulatory Commission,
III. To promote the development of market centres and wholesale markets,
IV. To boost the liquidity of the market, and
V. To manage the secondary capacity market of the related Integrated System.

335. In the same avenue, according to Article 65 of the HL, the Integrated National Natural Gas Transportation and Storage System may be composed of the following infrastructure:

I. Transportation Pipelines and Natural Gas Storage Facilities, and
II. Compression, liquefaction, decompression, regasification, and other natural gas transportation and storage facilities.

336. The classic System for transporting hydrocarbons between two given points is the pipeline (highly flexible carbon steel pipes), either buried on the earth's surface or at the bottom of the oceans. The transport capacity of gas pipelines depends on the pressure difference between their ends and their diameter (as this increases, so does the transport capacity).

337. The dry natural gas obtained from the processing complexes, extracted directly from fields, or imported, can be stored, transported, and distributed to the final users through pipelines.[99]

338. As mentioned above, since 1995, individuals may provide natural gas storage, transportation, or distribution services through pipelines, for which they require a permit granted by the RCE.

339. Under the provisions of the Energy Reform of 2013, to avoid vertical integration in the natural gas chain of value,[100] PEMEX transferred the ownership of its infrastructure for natural gas pipeline transportation[101] to National Centre of Natural gas Control (NCNC), as well as the associated permits to perform such activity.

340. Therefore, NCNC is the transportation licensee and the independent manager and administrator of Sistrangas, which comprises the National Gas Pipeline System and those private pipeline systems authorized by the RCE for tariff purposes.

341. Currently, these ducts are as follows: Tamaulipas Gas Pipeline, Gas Pipeline del Bajío, Gas Natural del Noroeste (formerly Transportadora de Gas Natural de Zacatecas), Gas Pipeline del Noreste (Los Ramones, Phase I), TAG Pipelines Norte (Los Ramones Phase II Norte) and TAG Pipelines Sur (Los Ramones Phase II Sur).[102]

342. Article 69 of the HL establishes that NCNC must propose a Five-Year Plan for the Expansion of the Sistrangas to the ME for its approval after receiving the FCE's technical opinion. This document contains the indicative planning proposed by CENAGAS and the projects of social coverage and those that the ME considers strategic to guarantee the efficient development of the System.

343. One of the key measures to develop a competitive natural gas market is implementing the capacity reserve for Sistrangas users to ensure open access on non-discriminatory terms and to identify infrastructure needs to meet the demand.

---

99. Pipeline transport is the most efficient way to transport natural gas, especially on a large scale. Due to its cost structure and the high initial investment required in fixed capital, which makes the cost of providing the service lower when there is only one carrier, this activity constitutes a natural monopoly. Given this condition, transportation permits involve the need for economic regulation, as well as the issuance of general terms and conditions, open access that is not unduly discriminatory, and the approval of rates by the FCE. Such rates emulate those that carriers would charge in a competitive environment.
100. That is, the same company performs processing, transportation, storage, distribution, and marketing activities.
101. The National Gas Pipeline System and the Naco Hermosillo System.
102. Secretaría de Energía, 'Plan Quinquenal de Expansión del Sistema de Transporte y Almacenamiento Nacional Integrado de Gas Natural 2015-2019', available at <https://www.gob.mx/cms/uploads/attachment/file/43397/Plan_Quinquenal_del_Sistema_de_Transporte_y_Almacenamiento_Nacional_Integrado_de_Gas_Natural_2015-2019.pdf>.

Chapter 7. Transport and Distribution

344. The HL establishes the principle of open and non-discriminatory access to the pipeline network. In this regard, Article 70 of this law provides in its first paragraph:

> Permit holders that provide transportation and distribution services to third parties using pipelines and hydrocarbon, oil, and petrochemical storage services shall have an obligation to provide open and non-discriminatory access to their facilities and services.

345. The same provision points out the rules that govern this access, which is as follows:

(a) Open access depends on the capacity in the systems in terms of the Regulation issued by the Energy Regulatory Commission.
(b) The Permit holders that have the capacity that is not contracted or that, being contracted, is not used shall make it public through electronic bulletins allowing third parties to take advantage of such available capacity.
(c) The use of this capacity requires prior payment of the authorized tariff and following the conditions for providing the service established by the RCE.

346. In addition to the above, the HL holds that providing services under the open access principle shall be subject to the general conditions issued by the RCE. The RCE will issue the regulations to which transportation and storage facilities will be considered of own use. In contrast, the ME will publish the public energy policy required to guarantee a reliable supply and open access to the pipelines.

347. The RCE issued general administrative provisions regarding open access and transportation services by pipeline and storage of oil and petrochemical products in 2016,[103] which were amended in 2018.[104]

103. Official Journal of the Federation 12 Jan. 2016.
104. Official Journal of the Federation 27 Aug. 2018.

Chapter 8. Supply to the Final Customers

348. The regulation of the supply of hydrocarbons to the final customer is poor in Mexico. The HL only mentions it in three precepts. Article 77 states that hydrocarbons must be supplied without alterations. In contrast, Articles 78 and 79 only refer to the RCE's power to issue Official Mexican Standards regarding hydrocarbons quality specifications and test, sampling, and verification methods applicable to qualitative characteristics, as well as volume in natural gas transportation, storage, distribution and, if applicable, retailing.

349. One of the significant changes introduced in this respect by the 2021 reform is that concerning permits for the commercialization of hydrocarbons, the authority that has issued a permit may temporarily occupy, intervene or suspend the facilities where the authorized activity is carried out in order to guarantee the interests of the nation. Such authority may contract productive state companies to carry out the activities whose performance had been authorized to private parties through a permit (Article 57).

350. Another important change introduced by the reform is that the Ministry of Energy and the Energy Regulatory Commission are empowered to revoke the permits for the commercialization of hydrocarbons when the holder carries out activities of transportation, storage, distribution or sale to the public of hydrocarbons, petroleum products or petrochemicals that have been acquired illegally or through the commission of the crime of smuggling (Article 56 section XI).

Chapter 9. Prices

351. In Mexico, no authority but the market defines the price of hydrocarbons. However, the administration does influence the determination of a maximum price for hydrocarbons.

Chapter 10. The Petroleum Fund

352. The Law of the Mexican Petroleum Fund for Stabilisation and Development establishes the rules for the creation and operation of the fund. The law has five chapters. The first chapter lays down general provisions and comprises Articles 1–4. The second chapter includes Articles 5–15 and deals with establishing the fund and integrating its committee. The third chapter covers the operation of the fund and consists of Articles 16–18. The fourth chapter deals with transparency and information on the fund's operations and consists of Articles 19–24. Finally, chapter five that is composed just by Article 25 refers to responsibilities and penalties.

353. Following Article 1 of the new Act, the fund is to receive, manage, invest and distribute the income from assignments and contracts that paragraph 7 of Article 27 of the Political Constitution of the Mexican United States refers to except for taxes.

354. However, Article 16 of the law orders to allocate resources of the Mexican Petroleum Fund under the following criteria:

(1) in terms of the Act of Hydrocarbons Revenue, the trustee will do payments under contracts and assignments referred to by paragraph 7 of Article 27 of the Political Constitution of the Mexican United States, no later than five bank business days after the Executive Director authorization;
(2) in terms of Title V of the Law of Federal Budget and Financial Responsibility, and according to the timetable established by the settlor, the trustee will do regular transfers of the fund's resources in the following order of priority:
   (a) to the *Fund for Stabilisation of Budgetary Revenue*;
   (b) to the *Fund for Stabilization States' Revenue*;
   (c) to The *Fund for* Exploitation *of Hydrocarbons*;
   (d) to the *Sectorial Fund CONACYT-Ministry of Energy-Hydrocarbons*, including amounts, according to the distribution determined by the technical committee intended to fund scientific research and technological development research institutes in hydrocarbons;
   (e) to the *Sectorial Fund CONACYT-Ministry of Energy for Energy-Sustainability*;
   (f) to *the Federal Treasury* to cover the costs of the Superior Audit of Federation for monitoring in the oil field; and
   (g) to *the Federal Treasury,* those necessary resources so as oil revenues addressed to cover the Federal Budget will remain unchanged at 4.7% of Gross Domestic Product (GDP). These resources include transfers to municipalities adjacent to the border or coastline by those who have physically carried the departure of hydrocarbons.

355. Once the payments and transfers referred to in sections (a) and (b) above, the trustee shall administer the remaining resources in the *Reserve of the Fund* to generate long-term savings from the Federal Government, including investment in financial assets; and

356. Resources corresponding to the Fund Reserve may be transferred in an extraordinary way to the Treasury of the Federation to cover the Budget of Expenditures of the Federation in terms of the Federal Budget Law and Fiscal Responsibility. The preceding, including transfers made from in accordance with the amounts approved by the Chamber of Deputies to use the resources when the Fund Reserve is more remarkable than 3% of the GDP.

Chapter 11. The Law of Revenue from Hydrocarbons

357. The Law of Revenue from Hydrocarbons (LRH) regulates the State's revenue from activities of exploration and exploitation of hydrocarbons carried out through assignments and contracts, as well as payments established by contracts with the Productive State Corporations or with private companies.

358. Article 2 of the law points out that Mexican State shall collect revenue from the activities of Exploration and Exploitation of Hydrocarbons, as follows:

(1) by contract, payment provided to the State in each agreement under this Act;
(2) by assignment, duties referred to in the third title of this Act; and
(3) the income tax causing contractors and assignees for the activities carried out under a contract or an assignment.

359. The following sections analyse these three sources of revenue.

§1. Income from Contracts

360. Title II of the LRH refers to state revenue arising from contracts with private companies in this field. Chapter I of this title regulates the income from licence agreements, contracts of shared utility and shared production, and contracts of service.

361. Regarding *licence agreements*, Article 6 of the Act states that the contractor must pay the Mexican State the following amounts:

(1) a bonus at signature;
(2) the contractual fee for the exploratory phase;
(3) royalties, determined under Article 24 of this Act; and
(4) Payment is determined in the contract considering the application of a tariff on the contract value of hydrocarbons.

362. In return, the mentioned legal provision states the contractor is entitled to receive the onerous transference of hydrocarbons once extracted from underground, under the condition that it has not failed in compliance with obligations adopted in the contract. In any case, the contractor is obliged to pay for hydrocarbons transferred to him.

363. In the case of *contracts for sharing utility,* following Article 11 of the LRH, contractors must pay to the Mexican State:

(1) the contractual fee for the exploration phase;
(2) royalties determined following Article 24 of this Act; and
(3) payment determined by applying a percentage to the operating profit.

364. In return, the contractor shall be entitled to recovery costs, subject to what Article 16 provides for, and to receive a payment that shall be the remnant of operating income after covering the fee mentioned in letter c of Article 11.

365. In contracts of sharing utility, contractors are obliged to deliver the entitled contractual production to the trader, which will provide the revenue from commercialization to the Mexican Petroleum Fund. The Mexican Petroleum Fund retains the income that corresponds to the Mexican State and pays those that fit the contractor.

366. In the case of *sharing production contracts,* Article 12 states that the contractor must pay the Mexican State the following amounts:

(1) the contractual fee for the exploration phase;
(2) royalties determined following Article 24 of this Act; and
(3) payment determined by applying a percentage to the operating profit.

367. In return, the contractor shall be entitled to recovery costs, subject to what Article 16 provides for, and to receive a payment that shall be the remnant of operating income after covering the fee mentioned in letter c of Article 12. In accordance with the nature of *sharing production contracts,* payments to contractors shall be in product, with a portion of contractual production of hydrocarbons. In the same way, payments to the Mexican State will be in the product.

368. Finally, in the case of *contracts for services* of exploration and exploitation of hydrocarbons, Article 21 of the law states that contractors are obliged to deliver the entire contractual production to the State and payments to the contractor will always be in cash. This provision adds that payment will be established to each contract considering the standards and practices of the industry.

369. In addition to the above, it should be clarified that Title II of LRH regulates two additional issues: (1) the contractual fees for the exploratory phase and (2) royalties.

370. Regarding contractual fees, Article 23 states that:

> The contracts shall provide a contractual fee for the exploratory phase to the Mexican State every month. Such fee has to be paid for those areas that are not in the production phase under the following payments:
>
> I. During the first sixty months of the contract, 1,150 Mexican MXN (76.50 US dollars) per square kilometre.
> II. From month sixty-one of the contract and after that 2,750 MXN (182.95 US dollars) per square kilometre.

371. In the cases of *royalties*, Article 24 of the Act states that contracts shall provide payments for each period. Such price in favour of the Mexican State is called *royalties*. The amount of royalties shall be determined for each type of hydrocarbon by applying the corresponding rate determined under sections I–III of this article, over the Contract Value of Oil, the Contract Value of Natural Gas and the Contract Value of Condensates according to the following:

1. To Petroleum Contract Value shall apply the following rate:
a. when the Petroleum Contract Price is less than USD 48 per barrel, 7.5%; and
b. when the Contract Price of Oil is greater than or equal to USD 48 per barrel:
Rate = [(0.125 x Contract Price of Oil) + 1.5]%
1. In the case of Contract Value of Natural Gas, applied the following rate will be:
a. in the case of Associated Natural Gas:
Rate = Contract Price of Natural Gas/100
a. in the case of Non-associated Natural Gas:
– when the Contract Price of Natural Gas is less than or equal to USD 5 per million BTU, 0%;
– when the Contract Price of Natural Gas is greater than USD 5 and less than USD 5.5 per million of BTU:
Rate = [(Contract Price of Natural Gas - 5) x 60.5/Contract Price of Natural Gas]%
– when the Contract Price of Natural Gas is greater than or equal to USD 5.5 per million of BTU:
Rate = Contract Price of Natural Gas/100
1. To Contractual value of Condensed the following rate will apply:
a. when the Contract Price of Condensed less than USD 60 per barrel, 5%; and
b. when the Contract Price of Condensed greater than or equal to USD 60 per barrel:
Rate = [(0.125 x Contract Price of Condensed) - 2.5]%

§2. Income from Assignments

372. In Mexican law, duties are those contributions that taxpayers must pay for using assets under the public domain or receiving public services.

373. Article 4 of LRH points out that without prejudice of causing other contributions, those conducting the activities of the hydrocarbon sector are subject to income tax on income obtained. Title III of the Act provides three new duties to be paid for those holding an assignment in this matter:

(1) the duty for sharing profit;
(2) the duty for extraction of hydrocarbons; and
(3) the duty for hydrocarbons exploration.

374. Article 39 defines the taxed activity of *duty over shared profit* as follows:

> Holders of assignments shall pay the duty annually for the shared profit by applying a rate of 65% to the tax base. The tax base results from taking away deductions allowed by Article 40 from the value of hydrocarbons extracted during the tax year in question.

375. From reading the quoted article, it is possible to assert that:

(1) The purpose of the tax is to tax the value of hydrocarbons extracted under an assignment.
(2) The taxpayer is the assignee.
(3) The tax base is the difference between the value of those hydrocarbons and authorized modifications.
(4) The rate is 65%.

376. Deductions are, by Article 40, the following:

1. about 100% of the original amount of investments for exploration, secondary recovery and non-capitalisable maintenance, in the year in which they occur;
2. about 25% of the original amount of investments for the development and exploitation of deposits of oil or natural gas, in each year;
3. about 10% of the initial amount of the investments in storage infrastructure and essential to the implementation of activities under the assignment, as pipelines, terminals or storage tanks, each year transport;
4. costs and expenses, considering for such purposes necessary for the removal of oil or natural gas deposits determined following Mexican Financial Reporting Standards, except investment expenditure referred to in sections I, II and III of this article. The only costs and expenses that are deductible will be exploration, transportation or delivery of hydrocarbons. Fees and expenses are deductible just when they have been paid into the period to which the payment corresponds, and
5. the right to extract hydrocarbons outlined in Article 44 of this law, actually paid during the corresponding period.

377. Under Article 39, this duty has to be paid no later than the last working day of March of the following year from which the payment corresponds. Payment has to be done by a declaration filed before the Tax Authority.

378. Article 44 of the Act defines the taxed activity of the *duty for extraction of hydrocarbons* by as follows:

> The assignee shall be required to pay monthly the right for hydrocarbons extraction, applying the applicable fee following Sections I to III of this article to the value of hydrocarbon extracted in the pertinent month.

379. The taxpayers of this tax are holders of assignments. The rate shall be defined in accordance with the prices of oil per unit as follows:

1. To the value of petroleum, the following rate will be applicable:
   a. when the price of oil is less than USD 48 per barrel of America, 7.5%; and
   b. when the price of oil is greater than or equal to USD 48 per barrel:

Rate = [(0.125 × Price of Oil) + 1.5]%

1. To the value of Natural Gas, the following rate will be applicable:
   a. in the case of Associated Natural Gas:

Rate = Price of Natural Gas/100

a. in the case of Non-associated Natural Gas:
   – when the price of Natural Gas is less than or equal to USD 5 per million BTU, 0%;
   – when the price of Natural Gas is more significant than USD 5 and less than USD 5.5 per million BTU:

Rate = [(Price of Natural Gas – 5) × 60.5]/ Price of Natural Gas

– when the price of Natural Gas is greater than or equal to USD 5.5 per million BTU:

Rate = Price/100

1. To the value of Condensed, the following rate will be applicable:
   a. when the price of Condensed less than USD 60 per barrel of America, 5%; and
   b. when the price of Condensed greater than or equal to USD 60 per barrel of America:

Rate = [(0.125 × Price of Condensed) – 2.5]%

380. Finally, Article 45 of the Act defines the taxable activity for the *duty over hydrocarbons exploration* in the following terms:

> The assignee is obliged to pay monthly hydrocarbon exploration right for the part of allocation area that is not in the production phase.

381. The taxed activities consist of exploration works carried out under an assignment. The taxpayer is the assignee. Article 45 asserts that this tax has to be paid following the following criteria:

(a) During the first sixty months of validity of the assignment, MXN 1,442.57 per km^2.
(b) Since the sixty-first month of validity of the assignment, MXN 3,449.63 per km^2.

§3. Tax on Activities of Exploration and Exploitation of Hydrocarbons

382. Different from what happens in the case of duties that are contributions in charge of those using natural resources under public domain. Generally, taxes are imposed on net profits from business, net gains and other income, and property and consumption. Article 54 of the LRH establishes tax that does not find into this category of taxation. According to this provision:

> Contractors and Assignees are required to pay the tax for hydrocarbon exploration and exploitation in those contractual or assignment areas, respectively.

383. As can be seen, taxable activity does not consist of obtaining a profit or owning patrimony or a consumption act but in exploration and exploitation activities. So this tax seems to fit better into the category of duties. However, duties never tax the use of private property assets. So, since exploration activities could affect subsoil and it is not an asset owned by the nation, this tax could result in unconstitutional.

384. By Article 55 this tax has to be calculated by applying to each square kilometre of the contractual or assignation area the following quotes:

(1) during the exploration phase, MXN 1,500 (USD 99.79); and
(2) during the extraction phase, MXN 6,000 (USD 399.16).

385. Article 57 states that the Fund for Oil Producers Local Entities and Municipalities shall be composed of revenue from this tax.

Part III. Regulatory Framework Concerning Coal

Introduction

386. The first coal production started in Mexico in 1884 in Coahuila State, placed in the north of the country. During those years coal production was mainly addressed to satisfy rail road's demand. By the end of the nineteenth century, the metallurgical and steel industries of the north of Mexico. Coal was gradually substituted by oil, particularly in the electricity generation industry, but it is still an essential input for steel and the mining–metallurgical sector.

387. Nevertheless, even during the growth years from 1902 to 1910, total production only summed a little over 10 million metric tons, and even in 1920, when Mexico's northern neighbour was extracting 600 Mt/year, Mexico was not able to surpass the 1.3 Mt, it had produced in 1910.

388. As a result of the Mexican Revolution, during the period 1911–1921, total coal production was only one million metric tons. This stagnation did not improve much during the next two decades.[105]

389. After several decades of low growth of coal production, by 1983, Mexican production of coal started to increase. In 2006, the national production was 11.5 Mt, 83% of the total production was addressed to satisfy the demand electricity generation plants (by that year, coal was responsible for 1.27% of electricity generation) whereas 17% to the steel industry. However, Mexico is far from self-sufficient, and by the same year, it was necessary to import 7.6 Mt to satisfy the internal demand.

390. In Mexico, there are three important coal regions. The most important is the Sabinas and Fuentes-Rio Escondido basin placed in the Centre-North of Coahuila and part of Nuevo Leon that has an extension of 12,000 km. This region produces 90% of the Mexican Coal. The second most important coal region is in Oaxaca in the South of Mexico, and the third one is in Hermosillo, Sonora in the North of the country.

105. Wallace, Robert Bruce, Coal in Mexico, available at www.economia.unam.mx last visit 5 Mar. 2012.

391. As mentioned, per paragraph 4 of Article 27 of the Mexican Constitution, coal is a mineral resource of subsoil – solid mineral fuels – that are owned by the nation and in consequence, their exploitation by private parties is possible by a concession granted by the Federal Government through the Ministry of Economy.

392. Under such a constitutional basis, the Mining Act of 1992[106] and its Regulation of 1999 rule coal energy.[107]

393. In Mexico, there are three important carboniferous regions. The most important of these is the basin of Sabinas and Fuentes-Rio Escondido at the centre-north of Coahuila and a small part of New Leon that covers almost 12,000 km^2 and produces 90% of the Mexican Carbon.

394. The second most important region, much more inferior, is placed in the northwest of Oaxaca, and the third most important is in the South of Hermosillo in Sonora. However, Mexico has reserves of 1.2 Gt that represents 0.1% of the total world reserves. Of these reserves, 869 Mt are bituminous carbon with minor metamorphosed anthracite, while 350 are sub-bituminous coals.

395. According to a study, after several decades of low virtual growing, by the 1990s, Mexican production of carbon grew up significantly to get 11.3 Mt in 2000.[108]

396. About 83% of the 11.5 Mt of carbon produced in 2006 was thermic carbon sub-bituminous addressed to carbon-electric plants and the rest, conquerable carbon mainly for the steel industry. However, production was insufficient to satisfy the growing demand from the FCE that had to import 7.6 Mt. It is expected that the carbon demand for electricity generation will grow 4.2% annually until 2030.

106. Official Journal of the Federation 26 Jun. 1992.
107. Official Journal of the Federation 15 Feb. 1999.
108. Robert-Bruce Wallace. El carbón en Mexico, at www.economia.unam.mx last visit February 2012.

Chapter 1. Constitutional and Legal Regime

397. According to paragraph 4 of Article 27 of the Mexican Federal Constitution:

> in the nation is vested with the direct ownership of all natural resources of the continental shelf and the submarine shelf of the islands; of all minerals or substances, which in veins, ledges, masses or ore pockets, from deposits of a nature distinct from the components of the earth itself such as solid mineral combustibles.

However, this constitutional provision authorized the Federal Government to grant concessions to exploit such resources to individuals or corporations constituted following Mexican laws.[109]

398. By these constitutional provisions, Mining Act passed by Federal Congress in 1992 (as amended in 2006) governs the issuance of mining concessions to private individuals and corporations. Article 40, paragraph VIII specifies that mineral coal in all its variations and its gas are governed by paragraph 4 of Article 27 of the Constitution.[110] In consequence, coal exploration, exploitation, and benefit are matters regulated by Mining Law, whereas transport and distribution do not have a specific legal statute.

399. Enforcement of Mining Law corresponds to the president through the Minister of Economy.[111] Reporting to the minister is the General Coordinator of Mining, with the rank of undersecretary, who oversees: (i) the General Directorate of Mining, in charge of applying the law; (ii) the General Directorate of Mining Promotion, whose charge is implicit in its name; (iii) the Mineral Resources Council,[112] responsible for geologic knowledge of the national territory; and (iv) the Trust for Mining Promotion, a lending institution.

---

109. *See* para. 6.
110. Exempted from the application of the law are: (i) oil and gas (a government monopoly, subject to their own law), (ii) radioactive minerals (also a government monopoly, with their own law), (iii) minerals dissolved or in suspension in underground water (subject to the laws on water), (iv) rocks or the result of their decomposition which may only be used as construction materials, (v) products resulting from decomposition of rocks that are mined in an open pit, and (vi) salt formed in basins that do not communicate with the sea.
111. Article 34 of Organic Act of Federal Public Administration points out the Ministry of Economy has the power to: (a) defining and conducting the national policy regarding mining issues (para. XXVII); (b) stimulating the exploitation of mining resources and administrate the mining register (para. XXVIII); (c) granting contracts, concessions, allocations, assignments, permits and authorizations in mining matters (para. XXIX).
112. Article 9 of Mining Act establishes that the Mineral Resources Council is a semi-autonomous organism focused on promotion to a better exploitation of mineral resources.

Chapter 2. Exploration and Exploitation

400. By Article 3, paragraph I of Mining Law, the activity of exploration includes those works or activities conducted in a piece of land to identify deposits of minerals or substances and to quantify and evaluate the reserves economically exploitable that such land contains,

401. In contrast, according to paragraph II of the mentioned provision, exploitation consists of those works and activities addressed at preparing and building the area that integrates the mineral deposit and separate and extract the mineral products and substances existing in that place.

402. The mining Act makes a distinction between concessions and allocations. In terms of Article 10 of this legal body, a concession issued by the Federal Ministry of Economics is necessary for private parties to conduct exploration and exploitation activities related to coal deposits. Mexican individuals, ejidos, agrarian communities, indigenous populations or communities, and corporations established under Mexican laws are eligible to apply for coal mining concessions.

403. Article 10 also establishes that allocations can be issued to allow the Mexican Service of Geology to identify and quantify the potential mineral resources of the country. In this case, the document containing the allocation title has to be published in the Official Journal of the Federation.

404. In other words, exploring the subsoil to identify the resources is an activity that both private parties may conduct through a concession or by the Mexican Service of Geology through allocation. If second then, the Government has two possibilities: reserve the identified resources to be exploited in the future or allocate them by a public bid, but if first, the holder of the concession is allowed to start exploiting the identified resources.

405. According to Article 15 of the Mining Act, concessions may last fifty years. This term can be extended for an additional equal period under the condition the holder applies for the extension of five years in advance of the expiration of the first period. By contrast, allocations have a duration of six years without the possibility of extension.

406. Mining Act establishes several rules that govern concessions issuance:

(1) Concessions are granted on mining lots. The sides of which perimeter must be astronomically oriented north-south and east-west and measure 100 m or a multiple thereof, except when adjoining lots (granted back when there were no orientation requirements) make this impossible.
(2) An exploration concession is granted to whoever first applies for it and meets the requirements of the law, the most important of which is that the claimed area is deemed to be 'free land'.

(3) Under the law, areas already covered by mining concessions or applications for mining concessions and mining reserves (locations where no mining may take place to reserve the minerals they contain for the future) are not free.
(4) When such circumstances disappear, the Federal Executive is obliged to declare the freedom of such area.

407. According to Federal Duties Act, concessionaries are obliged to pay duties for issuance of concessions and mining exploitation. Article 263 of the mentioned Act, concession and allocation holders are obliged to pay each six months of money for each hectare concessioner or allocate an amount from MXN 5.08 to MXN 111.17 (from USD 0.58 to USD 8.5). When concessions are issued through public bid, the winner has to pay economic compensation to the estate.

408. Concessionaires have the right to freely transfer their mining concessions and enter into any agreements in this regard, including the establishment of royalties. All agreements must be registered in the Public Registry of Mining. Any liens against concessions must also be registered if they are to be similarly effective.

409. The relationship between the concession holder and the landowner is one of the most critical issues of the mining legal regimen. Following the Mexican Constitution, just the subsoil and not the soil resources are properties of the nation. In this regard, the Mining Act rules that mining concessions do not automatically grant the right to enter or use the surface land of the mining lots, and much less another surface land.

410. Consequently, the concession holder needs to have the permission of the surface operator for this purpose. The Mining Law and its Regulations grant the concessionaire the right to request a temporary occupation or expropriation of the land or an easement of the way of roads, electricity lines, water pipelines, etc.[113] In these cases, the concessionaire has to pay compensation to the landowner.

113. Articles 55–58 of the Regulation under Mining Act.

Chapter 3. Benefit

411. Per Article 3, paragraph 3 of the Mining Law, benefit consists of those works for preparation, treatment or first-hand smelling of mineral products, in any of their phases, with the objective of recovery or to obtain mineral or substances and to elevate their concentrations or purity.

Chapter 4. Transport, Distribution and Consumption

412. The leading consumer of coal in Mexico is the Federal Commission of Energy that uses this hydrocarbon as a combustible for electricity generation. So, coal is transported through transportation bands from the mining to the electricity plant.

Part IV. Nuclear Power

Introduction

413. The development of nuclear energy in Mexico started in the 1970s, influenced by the international popularity of this novel energy source, particularly in the United States of America.[114] In 1975, Article 27 of the Mexican Constitution's reform added paragraph 7 that 'It also corresponds to the nation's exploitation of nuclear combustibles for nuclear energy generation and regulates its applications for any other purposes. Nuclear energy can only be used for peaceful purposes.'[115]

414. In that context, in 1976, Mexico built the unique Mexican nuclear plant in Laguna Verde Veracruz. This plant has two boiling water reactors that use dioxide of Uranic. Although Mexico has significant uranic reserves, given that the *Tlatelolco Treaty* forbids nuclear weapons (1969), it cannot use or export such resources. So, for Laguna Verde operation Mexico annually imports almost 25 tons from Holland and the United States of America. Laguna Verde can generate 1,365 NW that represents 2.6% of the installed capacity of Mexico's electricity sector generation.

415. Laguna Verde is owned and managed by FCE through the Division of Nucleon-electric plants. To guaranty Laguna Verde to meet international standards of nuclear security, The ME established the National Commission of Nuclear Security and Safeguards (NCNSS) in charge of enforcing standards in this area.

416. Apart from the constitutional principles, the Liability for Nuclear Damages Act of 1974 (Nuclear Liability Act)[116] and the Regulatory Act of Article 27 of the Constitution in Nuclear Matters of 1985 as amended in 1998 (Nuclear Energy Act) rules nuclear energy.[117]

417. The Nuclear Energy Act has multiple objectives of regulating exploration, exploitation and benefit of radioactive minerals and using of nucleon combustibles, uses of nuclear energy, technical and scientific research, nuclear industry, and all aspects related to it.

114. *See* Energy Nuclear (oil industry, basic petrochemistry and electricity generation are considered as strategic areas) Mexico at www.enegia-nuclear.net last visit 2 Feb. 2012.
115. Official Journal of the Federation 6 Feb. 1975.
116. Official Journal of the Federation 31 Dec. 1974.
117. Official Journal of the Federation 4 Feb. 1985 and 23 Jan. 1998.

418. Nuclear Liability Act aims to regulate civil liability from damages produced by nuclear reactors and the use of atomic combustibles substances and waste.

419. Nuclear energy has been considered as an alternative to substitute fossil fuels. Given that its operation does not generate CO_2 emissions, nuclear energy generation is one of the cleanest technologies. For instance, 30% of the electricity demand in Europe comes from nuclear energy that avoids 700 million tonnes of CO_2 emissions.

420. At present, official data shows that 439 nuclear reactors generate about 16% of electricity globally, and in nine countries, over 40% of energy production comes from nuclear energy.[118]Mexico's only built nuclear power plant is 'Laguna Verde', located on the Gulf of Mexico in Veracruz. This plant has two reactors with a capacity of 682.5 MW and contributes only 5% of electricity generation in the country.

421. However, nuclear power generation offers several drawbacks. First, minerals containing uranium and thorium are scarce, as is the case with fossil fuels.[119] Second, the construction of nuclear plants generates CO_2 emissions, and its operations generate radioactive waste. Thus nuclear energy is not clean. Third, uranium ores contain only 1 kg to 5 kg of metal per ton of ore, which would mean an excellent investment for removal.[120] Fourth, the risk of catastrophic nuclear accidents is always there.[121] Finally, research on nuclear energy can be used for military purposes.

422. Over the last two disadvantages of nuclear energy have signed various international treaties covered in the following sections of this chapter.

118. *See*: http://www.un.org/es/globalissues/atomicenergy/.
119. Wendt G, *La energía nuclear y su utilización para fines pacíficos*. París, UNESCO, 1955. p. 23. Disponible en http://unesdoc.unesco.org/images/0012/001283/128391so.pdf.
120. *Ibid.*, p. 27.
121. Entre los accidentes más catastróficos encontramos los acontecidos en la Unión Soviética en 1957, Gran Bretaña en 1957, Pennsylvania en 1979, Japón en 1981, Chernóbil, Unión Soviética en 1986 y Fukushima, en Japón 2011, entre otros.

Chapter 1. Constitutional Framework of Nuclear Energy

423. Mexican Constitution in Article 27, paragraph 7 sets up the basic principles regarding nuclear energy:

(1) First of all, using nuclear combustible for electricity generation is an exclusive activity of the nation.
(2) Second of all, using nuclear energy for any purpose different from electricity generation shall be regulated by the Federal Government.
(3) Third of all, nuclear energy just can be used for pacific purposes.

424. The first principle is also reflected in Article 28, paragraph 1, which states that: 'No constitute monopolies functions that the State exercised exclusively in the following strategic areas: postal, telegraph and radiotelegraphy; petroleum and other hydrocarbons; basic petrochemicals; radioactive minerals and nuclear power generation; electricity and activities specified in the laws enacted by the Congress of the Union ... .'

425. Section X of Article 73 also regulates the second principle. It holds: 'Congress has the power to legislate throughout the Republic on hydrocarbons, mining, chemicals, explosives, pyrotechnics, film industry, commerce, games of chance and sweepstakes, brokerage and financial services, electrical and nuclear energy, and to enact labour laws regulations of Article 123.'

426. The third principle adopts the provisions of international treaties to which Mexico is a party and which relate to the peaceful use of nuclear energy.

427. On 8 August 1963, Mexico signed the Treaty Banning Nuclear Weapons Tests in the Atmosphere, in Outer Space, and Under Water. According to this Treaty, the contracting parties undertake to 'prohibit, prevent, and not to conduct any test explosion nuclear weapons or any other nuclear explosion at any place under his jurisdiction or authority' (Article 1).

428. In 1967, Mexico was adopted in the Treaty for the Prohibition of Nuclear Weapons in Latin America and the Caribbean (LAC), better known as the Treaty of Tlatelolco. This international instrument consists of thirty-two items. It has been amended three times, the first in 1990 to add to the legal title of the Treaty the words 'and the Caribbean'; second, in 1991, to replace paragraph 2 of Article 25, which restricted the incorporation of new states to the Treaty; the third change took place in 1992 and consisted of a series of amendments to Articles 14, 15, 16 and 19.

429. According to Article 1 of the Treaty, the obligations to which the parties agree are as follows:

(1) Use exclusively for peaceful purposes the nuclear material and facilities under their jurisdiction, and to prohibit and prevent in their respective territories:

(a) To test, use, manufacture, produce or acquire n by any means whatsoever of any nuclear weapons, by themselves, directly or indirectly, on behalf of others or in any other form.
(b) To receipt, storage, installation, deployment and any form of possession of any nuclear weapon directly or indirectly, by themselves, on their behalf or otherwise.

(2) The contracting parties also undertake to refrain from engaging in, encouraging or authorizing, directly or indirectly, testing, use, manufacture, production, possession or control of any nuclear weapon or to participate in it in any way.

430. The Agency for the Prohibition of Nuclear Weapons in LAC is in charge of enforcing these obligations.

431. Another Treaty signed by Mexico concerning the peaceful use of nuclear energy is the Treaty on the Non-proliferation of Nuclear Weapons in 1968. In this agreement, the parties possessing nuclear weapons undertake not to pass them (Article 1), and if it is not, holders will not receive them (Article 2).

432. In 1971 another treaty was adopted: 'the Treaty on the Prohibition of the Emplacement of Nuclear Weapons and other Weapons of Mass Destruction on the Sea-Bed and the Ocean Floor and in the Subsoil thereof'.

433. The Treaty entered into force in Mexico on 23 March 1984. By Article 1 of the Treaty, the state parties undertake not to implant or emplace on the seabed and on the ocean floor and in the subsoil thereof beyond the outer limit of a seabed zone, as defined in Article II, any nuclear weapons or any other types of weapons of mass destruction as well as structures, launching installations or any other facilities specifically designed for storing, testing or using such weapons.

434. On 26 October 1979, the Convention on the Physical Protection of Nuclear Material was adopted, which entered into force in Mexico on 4 May 1988. This Convention has twenty-three articles *that regulate and establish liabilities related to safety transport of certain nuclear materials* used for peaceful purposes. Article 7 describes certain behaviours that should be considered crimes and should be punished by the domestic law of each State party. The Convention contains two annexes. Annexe I sets out the levels of physical protection to be applied in the international transport of nuclear materials, while Annex II has a classification of nuclear materials.

435. Finally, in September 1996, the Comprehensive Nuclear Test-Ban Treaty was accepted by the General Assembly of the United Nations. This Treaty is not yet in force since, according to paragraph 1 of Article XIV, it requires the ratification by the forty-four countries listed in Annex II. To date, only thirty-six have ratified it, including Mexico. Despite the above, the parties have held annual conferences in which, according to paragraph 2 of Article XIV, the controversial topic is the scope of paragraph 1 of Article XIV.

436. The Treaty establishes two essential obligations for countries party. The first obligation relates to the prohibition of any test explosion of nuclear weapons or any nuclear explosion at any place under its jurisdiction or control. The second prohibits encouraging performing any test explosion of nuclear weapons or other nuclear explosions or participating in any way. For the verification of compliance with these obligations, the creation of the Organization Comprehensive Nuclear-Test-Ban Treaty (OTPCEN in English) was established, including any verification system comprising: (a) an international monitoring system, (b) consultation and clarification, (c) site inspections and (d) measures of confidence-building.

Chapter 2. The Nuclear Law

437. The Regulatory Act on Article 27 of the Constitution in Nuclear Matters[122] has fifty-two articles. Its objective is to regulate exploration, exploitation and benefit of radioactive minerals and nuclear combustibles, nuclear energy uses, research in the nuclear field, and everything related to nuclear matters.

438. According to Article 5 of the mentioned Act, nuclear minerals are under the domain of the nation and, in its exploration, exploitation, and benefice, can be subject neither to concession nor to contract. Consequently, the ME can allocate these activities to the Council of Mineral Resources and the Council for Mining Foment.

439. However, Article 15 asserts that using nuclear elements for energetic purposes corresponds exclusively to the nation. In the same vein, electricity generation from atomic combustibles will be carried on exclusively by the FCE that has the power of designing and building nucleon-electric plants in consultation with the National Institute of Nuclear Research.

440. Finally, such provision holds that using nuclear reactors without energetic aims is only permitted to public sector and universities, institutes and authorized centres of research.

122. Official Journal of the Federation 4 Feb. 1985.

Chapter 3. The National Mineral Reserves Law

441. This Act was published in the Official Journal of the Federation on 26 January 1950. It consists of just sixteen articles and rules regarding uranium, thorium and other substances, which may be obtained cleavable isotope or radioactive material capable of producing nuclear energy (Article 1).

442. The law provides that the State will only exploit deposits through the Federal Executive or official institution that it determines (Article 3). According to the regulations under this law, the Mexican Geological Service shall exploit national mineral reserves containing radioactive substances (Article 3).

443. Whenever minerals are the exclusive property of the nation and their handling and extraction involves exploitation, use and management, the Act criminalizes different behaviours. Thus, Article 10 provides that imprisonment of one to ten years and a fine of MXN 100 to MXN 10,000 will be imposed to whoever:

(1) exploit in national mineral reserves, deposits of uranium, thorium and other substances which may be separated, produced or obtained cleavable isotope or radioactive substances that can produce nuclear energy; and
(2) trades, owns, extracts, refines, buys, disposes of, provides free transportation, and, in general, carry out any act of acquisition, extraction, refinement, supply or traffic of uranium, thorium, plutonium Pu-239 and other substances from which they can be separated, produced or obtained cleavable isotopes or radioactive substances that can produce nuclear energy, without being subject to provisions of this law.

444. Similarly, Article 13 states that imprisonment of six to twelve years and a fine of MXN 500 to 20,000 shall be imposed on those importing or exporting uranium, thorium, plutonium, Pu-239 and other substances that produce nuclear energy.

445. Finally, by Article 14, which fails to give notice ordering by Article 4 of this Act, within its established term, it will be liable of imprisonment from three days to one year and a fine of MXN 100,000.

446. Article 4 states that:

> Holders of mining concession, when – exercising their rights – found substances included into Article 1 of this law, and that possess those characteristics indicated by the regulation he holders of mining concessions, when exercising their rights discover the existence of the substances referred to in article 1 of this Law and that meet the characteristics indicated by the Regulation mentioned in the second paragraph of Article 2, will be at the disposal of the Federal Executive or the official institution designated for that purpose, giving the notice corresponding, within thirty days following the discovery.

Chapter 4. The Law on Civil Liability for Nuclear Damages

447. In 1974, the Law on Civil Liability for Nuclear Damage was published,[123] which aims to regulate civil liability for damage caused by nuclear reactors, nuclear fuel utilization, and substances and waste of these.

448. Following Article 3, paragraph (c) of the Law on Civil Liability for Nuclear Damage, nuclear damage includes:

> the loss of life, injuries and material damages that occur as a direct or indirect result of the radioactive properties or combination with the toxic, explosive or other hazardous properties of nuclear fuel or radioactive products or waste which are in a nuclear facility or nuclear hazardous substances that occur in it, under it, or are consigned to it.

449. Furthermore, the Act provides that the repair comment for nuclear damage compensation and notes will be ceiling the sum of MXN 100 million (Article 14). Following Francoz Rigalt,[124] this amount was established without measuring the severity of accidents. For instance, in the Chernobyl accident of 26 April 1986, the 'Total expenditures charged to the national budget of Ukraine for eliminating the consequences of the accident in the period from 1992 to 1996 alone exceed USD 3 billion.'[125]

123. Official Journal of the Federation 31 Dec. 1974.
124. Rigalt AF, *Los principios y las instituciones relativas al Derecho de la energía nuclear. La política nuclear*. México, UNAM, 1988, p. 44.
125. González J.A, 'Chernobil- Diez años después', en Boletín de la OIEA, 1996 p. 12, available at http://www.iaea.org/.

Part V. Renewable Sources of Energy

Introduction

450. In Mexico, energy production and supply depend primarily on fossil fuels (gas, oil, and coal). According to the *National Energy Balance* of 2018, hydrocarbons contributed 82.87% to the production of primary energy, almost two percentage points less than what was observed in 2017.[126] The participation of oil in that percentage was 62.4%, natural gas 19.7%, and coal contributed 4.3%; 10.4% of renewables, 2.4% of nuclear energy, and 0.8% of condensates. On the other hand, 85% of the gross domestic energy supply came from hydrocarbons, where natural gas and condensates represented 47% of the total supply, followed by oil and petroleum products with 38%.[127]

451. In addition, by the year 2020, Mexico's proven natural gas reserves amounted to 9,286 billion ft^3,[128] which, according to statistics from the ME, places Mexico in 22nd place among the countries with the largest natural gas reserves in the world[129]

452. Despite the above, Mexico is considered an importer of natural gas because it is still cheaper to buy it abroad than to extract and process it into the country. According to available data, 67% of the natural gas consumed in Mexico comes from the United States.[130] The extraction of natural gas in Mexico has decreased at a rate of 3.7% annually since a decade ago. In contrast, according to official data, during the last ten years, imports of this hydrocarbon from the United States of America to Mexico have tripled to reach 4.9 billion m^3 per day.[131]

126. Availabe at https://www.gob.mx/cms/uploads/attachment/file/528054/Balance_Nacional_de_Energ_a_2018.pdf.
127. Secretaría de Energía, 'Balance Nacional de Energía 2017' México, 2018, available at <https://www.gob.mx/cms/uploads/attachment/file/414843/Balance_Nacional_de_Energ_a_2017.pdf>. http://fundar.org.mx/mexico/pdf/Anuario2016corr.pdf.
128. Available at https://hidrocarburos.gob.mx/media/3652/reporte_reservas_recursos2020.pdf.
129. Available at http://sie.energia.gob.mx/movil.do?action=cuadro&cvecua=DIIE_C35_ESP.
130. Available at https://www.eleconomista.com.mx/empresas/Mexico-duplico-sus-compras-de-gas-natural-a-Estados-Unidos-en-un-lustro-20200226-0018.html.
131. Guerra Luz A & DiSavino S, *Rising U.S. Natural Gas Exports to Mexico Capped by Pipe Delays*' (2018), available at <https://www.reuters.com/article/us-usa-mexico-natgas/rising-u-s-natural-gas-exports-to-mexico-capped-by-pipe-delays-idUSKBN1KV2B3>.

453. It is difficult to reverse this trend. In fact, in 2019, Mexico imported 5.54 billion cubic feet of natural gas per day, and this is an increase of 3.4% compared to 2018.[132]

454. This scenario could only change to the extent that extracting natural gas from Mexican wells becomes more profitable.[133] The total liberalization of the natural gas industry through the constitutional reform of 2013, the secondary legislation that shapes it, and various administrative programmes enacted based on it seek precisely to achieve this goal.

455. In that regard, in 2016, the Mexican government issued the 'Public Policy for the Implementation of the Natural Gas Market' to establish a public policy that promotes the development of a competitive natural gas market, which will require the participation of private and public investment to generate multiple suppliers and buyers.[134]

456. Likewise, in 2018, the Mexican government announced a programme to renovate a series of the FCE plants close to leaving the System and rehabilitating hydroelectric plants.[135] However, while these efforts would help to improve the country's power generation from different sources, it is not enough to reduce the demand for natural gas.

457. On the other hand, it is worth noting that the new natural gas infrastructure began to take greater relevance after enacting the National Infrastructure Program 2014-2018.[136] This programme has as one of its main objectives 'To optimise the coordination of efforts for the generation of energy infrastructure, thus ensuring its adequate development to have sufficient, quality energy at competitive prices.' By 2019, according to official data, the country will have more than 16,000 kilometres of gas pipelines and twenty-four points of entry. In terms of distribution, there are 2.6 million users, which means 7% of the residential and commercial coverage[137]

458. Although it was expected that the signature by the Mexican government of the Kyoto Protocol in 1998, and especially its entry into force in 2005, would encourage use of renewable sources of energy,[138]currently, hydrocarbons continue to have majority participation in the gross domestic offer of primary energy.

---

132. Available at https://www.elfinanciero.com.mx/economia/importaciones-de-gas-natural-tocan-nuevo-record-en-2019.
133. This was stated by the engineer Saúl Cosme Pérez, general director of Graz & Grass, a 100% Mexican company, founded in 2001, specialized in the design, construction, and integral maintenance of natural gas networks.
134. Secretaría de Energía, 'Política Pública para la implementación del mercado de gas natural', 2016.
135. This programme, although announced by the President of the Republic, has not yet been issued.
136. Published into the Official Journal of the Federation in April 2014.
137. Available at: https://petroquimex.com/gasoductos-infraestructura-clave-para-el-desarrollo-economico-y-social-de-mexico/.
138. Mexico signed the Kyoto Protocol on 9 Jun. 1998, and ratified it on 7 Sep. 2000. The Protocol has been in force since 16 Feb. 2005.

459. Before the adoption of the Paris Agreement by the Mexican government, the contribution of renewable sources had been marginal and had been used mainly for heating or electricity generation purposes. However, Mexico has voluntarily committed to generating 35% of electricity by renewable sources in the mentioned international treated.[139]Currently, renewable sources provide 20.82% of the total energy consumed by the country, and the installed capacity to generate clean energy is 21,541.72 MW, which represents 29.09% of the national capacity. The contribution of the different renewable sources is as follows: hydroelectricity 12,628.6 MW that represents 17.06%, Wind 3,942.22 MV that represent 5.32%, geothermal 913.6 MW that represents 1.23%, bagasse 751.98 that represents 1.02%, photovoltaic 460.86 MW that represents 0.62% and finally biogas 88.67 MW that represents 0.12%.

460. In this way, renewable energy sources could supply enough energy to complement and gradually replace fossil fuels to satisfy Mexican demand in a cheaper and environmentally friendlier way.

461. Already Mexico ranks fourth in the capacity of generation of geothermal energy with 913.6 MW installed in the fields of Cerro Prieto (570 MWe), Los Azufres (248 MWe), and Los Humeros (94 MWe), Las Tres Vírgenes (10 MWe) and Domo San Pedro (10 MWe).[140] According to a Global Wind Energy Council (GWEC) report, among the Latin American countries, Mexico is one of the most promising countries for wind energy development. Its abundant wind resources have an estimated energy potential of 30,000 MW located in the region of the Isthmus of Tehuantepec, state of Oaxaca.[141] Similarly, the peninsulas of Baja California and Yucatan and the central region of Zacatecas have been identified as potential zones for wind energy generation.[142]

462. From September 2016 to June 2017, ten permits were granted to produce, transport and trade pure bioenergy: four went to small producers of biodiesel, two to produce anhydrous ethanol, two to market biodiesel, one to transport anhydrous ethanol and one to market anhydrous ethanol,[143] and two to generate electricity

139. 'Reporte de Avance de Energías Limpias Primer Semestre 2017', available at www.gob.mx/cms/uploads/attachment/file/279723/Informe_Renovables_2017_11122017.pdf.
140. *See*: http://www.cemiegeo.org/index.php/geotermia-en-mexico. This number represents 2.0% of the installed capacity. Additionally, a second stage of Los Azufres with a capacity of 107 MW is in construction and another one in Los Humeros with a capacity of 55 MW.
141. The most important developments have been advanced by the Federal Commission of Electricity with the installation of a 0.6 MW facility in the zone of Guerrero Negro, Baja California Sur, and the construction of the La Venta facility in Oaxaca with a capacity of 1.6 MW. According to data of the Regulatory Commission of Energy, there are three municipal projects and one industrial project authorized for the period 2003–2012 which will have an additional approximate capacity of 500 MW. The contribution of small aero generators and aero-water pumps installed throughout the country that annually generate more than 2 MW of wind electricity should also be taken into account. Finally, it is important to mention that the Federal Commission of Electricity is planning to build the second stage of La Venta with a capacity of 101 MW.
142. GWEC, 'Global Wind 2005 Report', available at www.gwec.net, 34–35.
143. https://www.gob.mx/cms/uploads/attachment/file/255394/5_Informe_SENER.compressed2.pdf.

based on the use of biogas produced by anaerobic fermentation of organic material at two water treatment plants. The last projects are in municipalities adjacent to Monterrey City and are currently in operation with an installed capacity of 10.8 MW and the ability to generate up to 54 GW/year. Additionally, there are forty-four permits to generate electricity of 391 MW.[144]

463. Although the above energy transition requires significant investments that the government must make under current constitutional and legal norms. However, governmental action focuses on investing in traditional energy than in renewable sources over the last decades. For instance, twenty new combined cycle energy plants were built over the previous ten years. In contrast, only one hybrid plant has been built in San Juanico, Baja California Sur.[145]

464. Replacing fossil fuels with renewable energy sources is not an easy job, but it could bring some benefits to the Mexican (carbon-based) economy.

465. The constitutional reform of 2013 also concerned the energy transition. Transitory articles seventeenth, eighteenth and nineteenth of the amendment provided a specific foundation to more relevant participation of clean energies into the energy matrix.[146] Under such a constitutional basis, in 2014, the Federal Congress passed the Geothermal Energy Law. The transition towards a low-carbon economy was also a concern shared by the CCGL[147] and the ETL.[148] In this regard, one of the objectives of the CCGL is to promote the transition to a competitive, sustainable and low-carbon economy resilient to extreme hydro-meteorological events associated with climate change.[149] In the same direction, the ETL pursues promoting a progressive increase of clean energies in the electricity industry. In CCGL, Mexico committed to reducing carbon emissions by 30% for 2020 and 50% for 2050.[150] ETL assumed increasing clean energies by 25% for 2018, 30% for 2021, and 35% for 2024.[151]

144. In 2003, the first project for generation of electricity from biogas generated by anaerobic fermentation of solid waste was started in Salinas Victoria, Nuevo León. This project has an installed capacity of 7.0 MW and a permit of generation of 58.2 GW/year. *See* Secretaría de Energía-GTZ, 'Energías renovables para el desarrollo sustentable en México'.
145. Available at www.cfe.gob.mx.
146. The Electricity Industry Law of 2014 (EIL) was designed to 'promote the sustainable development of the electricity industry and to guarantee its continuous, efficient and safe operation for the benefit of users, as well as compliance with principles of public and universal service, clean energies and pollutant emission reduction obligations'; this law contains just an incipient regulation on clean energies promotion.
147. Published in the Official Journal of the Federation 6 Jun. 2012.
148. Published in the Official Journal of the Federation 24 Dec. 2015.
149. Article two, s. VII of the Climate Change Law.
150. Second Transitory Provision of Climate Change Law.
151. Third transitory Provision of Energy transition Law.

§1. REGULATORY FRAMEWORK

466. Various laws regulate clean energies: the EIL, the General Climate Change Law, the Energy Transition Law, the Law for the Promotion and Development of Bioenergetics, and the Geothermal Energy Law. The following sections briefly describe each of these legal systems.

I. The Law for Energy Transition

467. The Law for Energy Transition of 2015 aims to regulate the sustainable use of energy and clean energies and pollutant emission reduction commitments of the electricity industry. The definition of sustainable use provided by the Law is not far from the one already offered by the Law for the Sustainable Use of Energy.

468. The Law, although new, does not introduce any innovative regulatory model. The legal system is structured around the idea of a Transition Strategy to Promote the Use of Cleaner Technologies and Fuels from which a National Program for the Sustainable Use of Energy and a Smart Grids Program derive.

469. In the third transitory article, the establishment of a goal to be achieved by the country in terms of clean energies. This provision holds: 'The Ministry of Energy will set as minimum goal participation of clean energies in the energy matrix of 25% for the year 2018, 30% for 2021 and 35% by 2024.'

470. The Law also establishes an energy transition financing scheme and a National Institute of Electricity and Clean Energy as a decentralized agency of the Federal Public Administration and an Advisory Council for Energy Transition.

471. The core of the Law is found in its Title Ninth – Articles 107–116 –. This regulates the so-called voluntary participation, since Article 107 postulates that excellence in energy efficiency is a voluntary certification and recognition process whose objective is to identify and promote products, equipment and buildings designed and conditioned to make sustainable energy use. To get this aim, this provision adds that excellence in energy efficiency consists of voluntary labelling of products and buildings that comply with the highest energy efficiency standards.

472. Certification and recognition of excellence in energy efficiency is the responsibility of the ME, with the technical support of the NCEUE. The NCEUE may request the support of the Ministry of Environment, the ME, and the Ministry of Agricultural, Territorial and Urban Development to evaluate and, if necessary, grant the recognition of excellence. The Law does not contemplate the procedure to obtain this recognition, but in its Article 109 it indicates that a regulation will be in charge of these aspects.

473. In addition, Article 111 of the Law states that the ME, through the NCEUE, may enter into voluntary agreements with participants from productive sectors that have significant energy consumption for each unit of physical production in order to reduce the energy intensity of their activities. These agreements should specify the energy intensity reduction target committed by the participants through this mechanism.

474. As is the case with the recognition of energy excellence, the Law does not regulate the requirements or procedure for the conclusion of these voluntary agreements. Still, it refers to the future publication of regulation on the subject.

475. Finally, Chapter V of Title Fourth of the Law refers to CECs stating in Article 68 that: 'to promote the growth of clean energies referred to by this Law and in the terms established by the Law of Electricity Industry, the Ministry shall set obligations to acquire clean energy certificates'.

476. According to section V of Article 3 of the Law in question, a CECs is a title granted by the RCE per the provisions of the Electricity Industry Act, which does not define this instrument. However, the Law neither clarifies who is in charge of this obligation nor the procedure and requirements for acquiring these certificates, although it does dedicate several provisions to regulate the creation and operation of the Public Registry of CECs.

477. Regarding obligated subjects, Article 123 of the Law of Electricity Industry states:

> The Suppliers, the Qualified Market Participating Users and the End Users that are supplied by the isolated supply, as well as the holders of the Legacy Interconnection Contracts that include Loading Centers, whether public or private, will be subject to the fulfilment of the Clean Energy obligations in the terms established in this Law.

478. On the other hand, Article 3, section VIII of the Law of Electricity Industry states that a CECs is a title issued by the RCE that accredits the production of a determined amount of electricity from Clean Energies and that serves to comply with the requirements associated with the consumption of load centres

479. This Act refers to CECs in Articles 121–129. The legislative technique of the law is not appropriate. According to Article 21 of the law mentioned above, the obligation to acquire CECs does not derive from any legal system.

480. This provision states in its second part that:

> The Ministry shall establish the obligations to acquire Clean Energy Certificates and shall implement the other mechanisms required to satisfy the policy on this matter, and may enter into agreements that allow their homologation with the corresponding instruments of other jurisdictions.

481. Nevertheless, what the provision mentioned above tries to indicate is that the Ministry will establish the requirements for granting the certificates and not the obligation to obtain them. However, this contradicts the provisions of the new law that refers to the regulation for such purposes.

482. Similarly, Article 124 of the Electricity Industry Act is susceptible to the constitutionality judgment since it states that:

> In the first quarter of each calendar year, the Ministry shall establish the requirements for the acquisition of Clean Energy Certificates to be fulfilled during the three years following the emission of such provisions and may specify conditions for subsequent additional years. Once the requirements for a future year are established, they will not be reduced.

483. It seems to the authors to be a failure of the Law since the requirements should be established in the body of the legal level itself and not left to the authority's discretion.

484. The regulations to the Act should therefore fill this and other gaps.

II. The Law for Promotion and Development of Bioenergetics

485. Biofuels are also a possibility of expansion of renewable energies. For example, in 2011, the first plant of non-food biodiesel started operations in the State of Chiapas[152] from the culture of 'jatropha curcas' or piñón[153] for its use in the public transport system city of Tapachula, Chiapas.

486. The Law on the Promotion and Development of Bioenergy aims to promote and develop bioenergy to contribute to the agricultural sector's energy diversification and sustainable development (Article 1).

---

152. Biodiesel is produced from oleaginous plants such as safflower, soybeans, sunflower, jatropha or palm oil, used cooking oil or animal fats. Depending on its quality, it can be used directly in diesel engines or combined with fossil diesel to increase the lubricity of the latter, since biodiesel tends to be denser.
153. Jatropha is a Mexican plant, also known as piñon or piñoncillo. It is found in tropical and semi-tropical climates, it is a shrub-tree that can reach a height of 1 to 8 m and grows at altitudes ranging from 5 to 1,500 m above sea level. It grows in poor and sandy soils, is resistant to drought and the seed has an important content of protein and fat, it is necessary to clarify that to obtain adequate yields to make a profitable project, in good lands and without water limitations can be obtained 5 tons of seed per hectare, and in marginal lands only 1.5 tons of seed per hectare can be obtained, and in marginal lands only 1.5 tons per hectare.

487. This law defines bioenergy fuels as those obtained from organic materials generated by agriculture, forestry, aquaculture, fishing, domestic, industrial and commercial waste, microorganisms and enzymes, and their derivatives produced by sustainable technological processes.

488. Under Article 24 of this law, the implementation of activities and services related to the production, storage, transport, distribution and marketing of bioenergy products requires prior obtaining a permit following section III of Article 12 to grant the ME. By this provision and section IV of Article 12 of the Spoils Act, ME is empowered to identify when the permit referred not required by the emission of criteria and guidelines for granting permits.

489. The Act creates in Article 8 a Commission of Bioenergy, which will be composed of the heads of Ministry of Agriculture and Rural Development, ME, Ministry of Environment, the SE and the Ministry of Finances.

490. Under this provision in 2008, the Inter-ministerial Commission for the Development of Bioenergy was also established.[154]

III. The Law of Geothermal Energy

491. The Constitutional base for the Law of Geothermal Energy is in transitional provision number 18. Paragraph 2 of Transitional provision number 18 of the Constitutional Reform of 2013 orders the Federal Congress to pass a law on geothermic energy. On such a constitutional basis, Federal Congress passed the new Geothermal Energy Act in August 2014.

492. This law comprises sixty-six provisions that regulate recognition, exploration and exploitation of geothermal energy activities of recognition of geothermal energy resources (Article 1). The law defines recognition as the activity aimed at identifying those areas of Mexican territory that can be sources of geothermal resources. Exploration consists of works on the surfaces or into the subsurface aimed at proving the existence of geothermal resources. Finally, exploitation is the series of activities addressed to obtain energy from the subsurface heat.

493. According to the new legal body, exploration and exploitation activities can be carried out by private companies, the FCE, or other State Productive Corporations, whereas recognition activities are reserved to the FCE.

494. Recognizing geothermal resources only requires a registration granted by the ME (Article 8). For exploration activities, it is necessary to obtain a permit from the mentioned authority (Article 12). Finally, to conduct exploitation activities, it is

154. On 31 Dec. 2012, the Internal Regulations of the Inter-Secretarial Commission for the Development of Bioenergy were published in the Official Journal of the Federation, the purpose of which is to establish the basis for the organization and operation of the Commission.

required of a concession granted by the ME (Article 26). According to this article, the concession shall be issued for thirty years, and they can be renewed.

495. The law also established that use of the surface for geothermal energy generation purposes is preferment over any other use of the soil (Article 4).

496. Perhaps the main critique that the new law deserves is that, different from what happened in oil hydrocarbons, the Mexican Constitution does not consider geothermal resources a national property. So, there is no foundation to require a concession for their exploitation.

IV. The Energy Industry Law

497. The IEL includes an innovative mechanism aimed at promoting the energy transition: the Clean Energy Certificates (CECs).

498. A CEC is, per Article 3, section VIII of the EIL, a certificate issued by the ERC that certifies the production of a certain amount of electricity from clean energy sources. CECs serve to meet the requirements associated with the consumption of load centres.[155] According to Article 83 of the EIL Regulation, these certificates are disruptive to achieving electricity generation participation from clean energy sources at the lowest possible cost based on market mechanisms.

499. The obligation to acquire CECs was first established by Article 121 of the EIL[156] and later reaffirmed by Article 68 of the ETL.[157] According to the EIL, all electricity suppliers are obliged to cover a certain percentage of their demand with clean energies, and CECs certify compliance with this obligation. Article 123 of the EIL states that the following are obliged to acquire these certificates: (a) Suppliers; (b) Qualified Market Participant Users; (c) Final Users supplied by isolated

155. A load centre is defined by Art. 3 s. VII of EIL as those 'Facilities and equipment that, at a given site, allow an final user to receive the electricity supply. The load centres will be determined at the metering point of the energy supplied'.
156. Under Art. 121 of the LEI, 'The Secretariat shall implement mechanisms to comply with the policy on diversification of energy sources, energy security and the promotion of Clean Energy sources. The Secretariat shall establish the obligations for acquiring Clean Energy Certificates and shall implement other mechanisms required to comply with the policy in this area and may enter into agreements that allow its homologation with the corresponding instruments of other jurisdictions"'.
157. In this sense, Art. 68 of the LTE states, 'To promote the growth of Clean Energy referred to in this Law and under the terms established in the Electricity Industry Law, the Secretariat will establish obligations to acquire Clean Energy Certificates. To maintain equal competition, these obligations shall apply to goods consumed in a national territory whose production process is energy-intensive.'.

electricity supply; and (d) Holders of Legacy Interconnection Contracts[158] that include load centres, whether public or private.[159]

500. According to its energy production, every clean energy generator is entitled to CECs and can subsequently sell them to suppliers on a free-market basis. In this way, the price of a certificate depends on supply and demand.

501. The mandatory minimum percentage of certificates that a supplier must hold increases year by year: for 2019, the rate was 5.8%, and for 2020, it was 7.4%. In addition, non-compliance is punished by a fair 6 to 50 Mexican minimum salaries (USD 46.84 to USD 357) for each MW/h of non-compliance in the procurement of CECs.

502. In October 2014, the Ministry of Energy (ME), based on Articles 121, 122, 123, 125, and 126 of the EIL, issued the *Guidelines establishing the criteria for granting clean energy certificates and the requirements for their acquisition.*[160] According to this document, those clean power plants that came into operation after 11 August 2014 would be entitled to receive CECs for twenty years. Then, legacy plants, that is to say, plants that started operations before this date,[161] would not be eligible for CECs unless they had made investments to increase their clean energy production. Furthermore, CFE was obliged to purchase CECs in the market or pay the corresponding fine under this rule.

503. This rule changed on 28 October 2019, when the ME published in the Official Gazette of the Federation the Agreement amending the Guidelines that establish the criteria for the granting of Clean Energy Certificates and the Requirements for their acquisition, published on 31 October 2014.[162] According to sections I and II of numeral 4 of the new Guidelines:

> 4. Eligible to receive CECs for a period of up to twenty years shall be clean generators representing:

---

158. The Electricity Industry Law of 2014 created two parallel legal regimes: (i) a so-called legacy or grandfathered regime granting vested rights to projects holding a power permit or an application filed with the Mexican Energy Regulatory Commission (CRE) before the enactment of the Electricity Industry Law, and (ii) an 'electricity market' regime under which projects are subject to burdensome regulations affecting congestion, financial transmission rights, and transmission and distribution fees. So, a legacy interconnection contract is the interconnection contract or power purchase commitment contract for small producers concluded or to be concluded under the conditions in force before the entry into force of this Law.
159. CELs can also be acquired voluntarily by registering as a Voluntary Entity in the Clean Energy Certificates and Compliance Management System.
160. Published in the Official Gazette of the Federation on 31 Oct. 2014.
161. A Legacy Power Plant is a Power Plant that, at the entry into force of the LIE, is not included in a permit to generate electricity under the modality of self-supply, cogeneration, small production, independent production or own continuous uses, and: (a) is owned by State agencies, entities or companies and is in operating conditions, or (b) whose construction and delivery has been included in the Federal Expenditure Budget in the modality of direct investment.
162. Published in the Official Gazette of the Federation on 28 Oct. 2019. This Agreement in turn was amended by another Agreement of 10 Dec. 2019.

i. Clean Power Plants that entered into operation after August 11, 2014.
ii. Legacy Power Plants, as provided for in the Electricity Industry Law, generate electricity from Clean Energy sources.

504. Under the new wording of the provision mentioned above, clean legacy power plants can receive CECs for their energy production. However, since the CECs requirements for 'obligated participants' were not increased, this modification will cause an oversupply of these instruments in the market.[163] In other words, this change allowed CFE's hydropower plants to issue CECs, which would devalue prices to almost zero and discourage clean generation. Therefore, CFE no longer needs the auctions and no longer must pay penalties.

505. The change also decreases the return on investment in clean technologies, restricting the clean electricity industry's development. Furthermore, the guidelines' shift creates uncertainty for investors, which does not help reverse the economy's stagnating trend.

§2. Solar Energy

I. Introduction

506. Solar energy is a form of renewable energy generated through the transformation of solar radiation, by various types of solar panels, into electrical energy. Solar energy is one of the most developed and widely used renewable energy sources in the world. There are three types of solar energy: thermal solar energy, photovoltaic solar energy and passive solar energy. The first type of solar energy utilization, thermal solar energy, harnesses solar radiation to generate thermal (caloric) energy and is predominantly used to heat water or other fluids. Photovoltaic solar energy relies on photovoltaic cells (in photovoltaic panels) to convert sunlight directly into electricity. The electricity generated through these panels can be fed into the electricity grid or used directly, if generated by a prosumer. Passive solar energy is materially different from thermal solar energy and photovoltaic energy and refers to the utilization of solar radiation without other human technology. To work with the area's climate, passive solar energy employs specialized architectural designs, using special materials for conserving heat or light provided by the sun, thus maximizing natural energy use. It is usually a key consideration in eco-design.

507. Mexico is located within the 'solar strip' – 'the series of countries (60 in total) that absorb greater amounts of solar radiation, located between the Tropics of

163. J. Vazquez Perez, 'Cambio De Reglas En La Adquisición De Certificados De Energías Limpias: Consecuencias De La Política Eléctrica' (Ciep.mx, 2021) https://ciep.mx/cambio-de-reglas-en-la-adquisicion-de-certificados-de-energias-limpias-consecuencias-de-la-politica-electrica/, accessed 9 Mar. 2021.

Cancer and Capricorn'. Mexico has been identified as a top-three country in terms of solar radiation received, trailing only China and Singapore.

508. According to official data, the average solar radiation in Mexico is 5.56 kWh/m^2 per day. However, in Mexico, photovoltaic energy is still underutilized, with solar energy representing just 1% of primary energy generation. Historically, photovoltaic technology was concentrated in remote areas that were not connected to the existing electricity grid. In recent years, however, most newly installed photovoltaic capacity is connected to the electricity grid.

509. Solar radiation is beginning to play an essential role in electricity generation worldwide, and Mexico is no exception. This is mainly due to the rapidly decreasing electricity generation costs through solar radiation, which has allowed unsubsidized photovoltaic solar energy generation to compete with non-renewable electricity generation.

510. Since 2011 (marked by the publication of the First Interconnection Contract for Small Scale Solar Power Source and the entry into operation of the first large-scale photovoltaic power plant in Mexico), installed solar electricity generation capacity has risen from 18.5 MW in 2007 to 2,104 MW in 2018, with a total of thirty-eight photovoltaic plants distributed in twelve local states. This increase has been reinforced by the significant growth of small and medium scale prosumers through 'Legacy Interconnection Contracts', which have since 2010 observed significant growth rates. The huge potential of solar energy was reflected in the results of the first, second and third long-term renewable power auctions.

511. For instance, the second auction, in which companies sought to win long-term power purchase agreements for renewable energy generated, resulted in 54% of the 8.9 TWh capacity being allocated to solar energy projects. The capacity up for grabs in this auction represented approximately 3% of Mexico's total annual electricity generation capacity.

512. 65,400 MW of solar generation capacity was expected to come online by the end of 2019, with the new solar plants realized as a result of the first, second and third long-term renewable power auctions set to contribute 1,691 MW, 1,853 MW, and 3,040 MW respectively. As a result of the Mexican government's decision to cancel the fourth auction, however, this capacity was not realized. The use of solar energy to generate electricity through photovoltaic technology can be divided into two main areas: large-scale generation projects and systems small and medium scale photovoltaic, distributed in places of consumption. In Mexico, solar energy is predominantly used for thermal applications (heat generation). The industrial sector trails the residential and commercial sectors in the consumption of solar energy.

II. Legal Framework

513. Mexico has yet to adopt a specific legal framework governing solar energy. Currently, photovoltaic electricity is regulated by both the legal framework for renewable energy and the legal regime for the electricity industry. These will be discussed in the following sections.

514. The use of solar radiation to generate electricity is regulated through the Law of Energy Transition, the Climate Change Law, and the Electricity Industry Act. The Law of Energy Transition aims to encourage the sustainable use of energy and stipulates the obligations of the Mexican government regarding clean energy and the reduction of greenhouse gas emissions from the electricity-producing industry. The Law of Energy Transition identifies funding schemes for implementing actions to promote the energy transition, the development of clean energy infrastructure, and the sustainable use of energy as the most important instruments to realize this goal. In addition, Articles 68–74 of the Law of Energy Transition govern the obligation to acquire CECs, the requirements to reach them, and how the RCE establishes and manages the Public Register of CECs.

515. Meanwhile, the Electricity Industry Act regulates the generation, transmission, distribution, and electricity supply explicitly. The Electricity Industry Act also seeks to promote the sustainable development of the electricity-producing industry and guarantee its continuous, efficient, and safe operation for the benefit of customers. Rolled into this is the duty to fulfil the obligation to provide public and universal service and to reduce emissions. The stimulation of renewable energy generation is mentioned in Chapters I and III of Title Four of the Electricity Industry Act. It is established that the Ministry bears responsibility for setting out policies and strategies to ensure electricity supply to the public and promote renewable energy technologies. Thus, both the Law of Energy Transition and the Electricity Industry Act complement one another to bring the energy transition to Mexico. In both cases, Clear Energy Certificates are the main instrument to get such a goal. Finally, the Climate Change Law also aims to promote the transition towards a competitive, sustainable, low-carbon emissions and resilient economy. The law identifies renewables as a means of mitigating climate change. The following subsections analyse the legal regime applicable to photovoltaic energy as established by the Law of Energy Transition, the Electricity Industry Act and the Climate Change Law.

III. Solar Energy Activities

A. Generation

516. The Electricity Industry Act also regulates the different links of the electricity value chain, regardless of the energy source. Therefore, all solar energy value chain stages are subject to the general regime established by Electricity Industry Act to govern the electricity industry. Article 4 of the Electricity Industry Act states that electricity supply is a 'service of public interest'. That electricity generation is to occur under 'a regime of free competition'. Under such basis, Article 17 of the Electricity Industry Act sets out that 'power plants with a capacity equal to or above 0.5 MW and power plants of any size represented by a generator in the wholesale electricity market' must obtain permission from the RCE. Therefore, consent is not required for photovoltaic plants with capacities below 0.5 MW, as they do not operate in the wholesale electricity market.

517. Furthermore, an exemption is granted for installations that exist solely for self-use in the event of an interruption of electricity supply (or other emergencies). Per Article 3(XXV) of the Electricity Industry Act, according to fraction XXV of Article 3, the owner or possessor of such an installation is classified as an 'Exempt Generator'. Article 130 of the Electricity Industry Act states that, to obtain the permit, it is necessary to file a request under the RCE, including the following information: accreditation of the payment of fees under the terms established by Mexican tax law; information regarding its corporate purpose; legal, technical and financial capacity, and; a description of the project. Per Article 21(V) of the Regulation of the Electricity Industry Act, 29 the following information must be given by those seeking a generation permit: (a) the location of the Power Plant; (b) the estimated annual capacity and generation of the plant; and c) the type of technology and, when appropriate, the primary fuel. The decision to grant a permit is at the sole discretion of the RCE. Finally, it is important to mention that Article 8 of the Electricity Industry Act establishes the principle of legal separation: 'The generation, transmission, distribution, commercialization and primary inputs for the electricity industry will be carried out independently of each other and under conditions of strict legal separation'. An understanding of what is meant by 'commercialization' is the focus of the following subsection.

B. Transmission and Distribution

518. Electricity transmission and distribution activities are the sole reserves of the Mexican state, as stated in the Mexican Constitution. The Electricity Industry Act states that transport and distribution of electricity are activities conducted by 'Productive State Corporations' or their subsidiaries. Article 5 of the Law of the Federal Electricity Commission sets out the principle aim of the body as being 'to provide, following applicable law, the public service of transmission and distribution of electricity, on behalf of the Mexican State'. Under the principle of strict separation, solar electricity generators are therefore prohibited from transmitting and distributing electricity themselves. However, this does not represent a legal problem for solar energy's participation in the energy market. Article 33 of the EIL stipulates that carriers and distributors are obliged to interconnect their networks to power plants (including photovoltaic installations) and to end users upon request. This must be done 'under conditions that are not unduly discriminatory, where technically feasible'. As a result of this (and the legal separation provisions), photovoltaic installation owners and operators should not suffer from discrimination from entrenched competitors when bringing their electricity to the market.

C. Commercialization

519. The commercialization of solar energy Per Article 45 of the Electricity Industry Act, commercialization of electricity entails one or more of the following activities: I. To provide electricity supply to final users; II. To represent exempt generators in the wholesale electricity market; III. To carry out the transactions in

Article 96 of this law, in the wholesale electricity market; IV. To enter into the contracts referred to in Article 97 of this law with generators, traders, and qualified users participating in the market; V. To acquire transmission and distribution services based on regulated rates; VI. To acquire and dispose of related services not included in the electricity market, with NCEC mediation; and VII. Any others determined by the Regulatory Commission of Energy. While Article 8 of the Electricity Industry Act appears to prohibit electricity generators (including photovoltaic plant owners and operators) from carrying out any commercialization activities, Article 19, which is itself closely linked to Article 45, appears to give generators specifically some room for manoeuvre. According to Article 19 of the Electricity Industry Act, generators may carry out the commercialization activities referred to in Article 45 of this law [above], except for the provision of electricity supply. This implies that despite the strict legal separation, generators may carry out the commercialization activities listed in Article 45(II–VII). Though Article 4 of the Electricity Industry Act states that selling electricity is done under 'a regime of free competition', Article 45 clarifies that permission from the RCE will nonetheless be required in any instance where electricity is supplied to a final customer. Furthermore, per Article 8, transactions made between generators and those carrying out commercial activities (such as electricity supply) are subject to the RCE's rules.

§3. WIND ENERGY

520. Wind energy is obtained by harnessing the wind; electricity is produced from installed wind turbines, exploiting the kinetic energy of the air.

521. To better use this energy, it is necessary to consider several factors such as the orography, the behaviour of the wind, and the communities near where the wind farms are to be installed.

522. Wind energy in Mexico has grown exponentially over the years. For example, between 2005 and 2015, it increased its installed capacity by 104.7% annually, the highest growth among renewable energy sources developed in the country. Mexico has an excellent wind energy potential; as of 2019, it had more than 6,237 megawatts of wind energy installed, ranking 16th in the world in this area, and in 2020 it will surpass the 7,000-megawatt mark.[164]

523. By the end of 2021, the country will reach an installed capacity of 7,800 megawatts, which will imply an annual increase of 9%. However, this will be all the increase expected throughout the current administration, given the conditions of legal uncertainty, such as a total of 400 appeals in the process against the reform to the EIL, and lack of robustness in the national transmission network.[165]

---

164. *See*: https://energyandcommerce.com.mx/potencial-de-la-energia-eolica-en-mexico-2021/.
165. *See*: https://www.eleconomista.com.mx/empresas/Crecimiento-eolico-en-Mexico-se-frenara-durante-la-presente-administracion-AMDEE-20210518-0057.html.

524. The state with the greatest wind potential within the Mexican Republic is Oaxaca, specifically the Isthmus of Tehuantepec, with an annual capacity to supply 18 million users. The Isthmus of Tehuantepec is located in the narrowest part of the Republic, which leads to the wind behaviour to be high-speed currents, reaching up to 10 m/s. In this example, it is clear that the first two fundamental requirements for the correct use of wind energy, orography and wind behaviour, are fulfilled. Still, as for the nearby communities, the conflict in the Isthmus of Tehuantepec has not subsided. Since 2009, contentions have been documented between wind energy companies and local inhabitants, who complain about the companies' abuse and disagree with the installation of wind farms.

525. Regarding the legislation that regulates the generation, use and exploitation of wind energy and the necessary permits to carry out these activities, Mexico does not have any specific law. The Electric Energy Law and the Law for the Use of Renewable Energies and the Financing of the Energy Transition regulate these activities.

§4. Hydropower

526. There is an excellent debate if hydroelectric energy is a renewable source of energy since, once the dam is built, it is practically renewable energy. The environmental impact of the reservoirs is enormous.

527. In Mexico, there are 86 hydroelectric plants with a total installed capacity of 12,642 MW, which generated 31,848 GWh during 2017, equivalent to 10% of the entire generation during that year. The five largest hydroelectric plants are located three in Chiapas, one in Michoacán and one in Nayarit

528. The Political Constitution of the United Mexican States states that the nation owns river waters. Therefore, using these waters to generate electricity requires a concession granted by the NWC.

529. The National Waters Law regulates the use of national waters in generating electric energy in Articles 78–81. By Article 80 of the National Waters Law, the exploitation, use or exploitation of national waters to generate electricity power requires a concession granted in terms of the applicable law on the matter. This concession is not necessary to exploit, use, or exploit national waters on a small scale for hydroelectric generation.

530. In addition, generating electricity by this means requires permission granted in terms of the EIL and the authorization of environmental impact granted in terms of the General Law of Ecological Balance and Environmental Protection.

§5. HYDROGEN

531. Hydrogen is the most abundant chemical element on earth, with high energy density, found naturally in a gaseous state, but is mainly combined with various elements such as oxygen, forming water molecules. Hydrogen is considered an energy vector. When the hydrogen extraction process is carried out, part of the energy used in this process is stored in the hydrogen molecules so that it can later be transported and used, either as electricity or as fuel, among others.

532. By its nature, hydrogen is colourless, but it is assigned different colours associated with how the hydrogen is extracted and therefore how 'clean' it is.

533. Black hydrogen is obtained from coal gasification, so CO_2 is released in its production; grey hydrogen is obtained from methane and emitting CO_2; turquoise hydrogen is obtained mainly from natural gas; blue hydrogen is also obtained from fossil fuels its difference is that CO_2 emissions are captured. On the other hand, hydrogen produced without emitting CO_2 is pink hydrogen, which is obtained with nuclear energy, and green hydrogen, the cleanest, which is obtained from water. The energy used in the extraction process is renewable.

534. The energy obtained from hydrogen is clean, safe and sustainable; many countries are beginning to bet on a hydrogen economy, hoping to make it the primary fuel used and thus omit CO_2 emissions to the environment. The problem we are currently facing is that obtaining green hydrogen is costly, so the most significant step to start this transition is to invest in infrastructure to lighten its price. This transition from a fossil fuel system to a hydrogen system will naturally be gradual and take many years; the technological challenges to be faced are significant but not impossible.

535. In Mexico, we are up to fifteen years behind countries such as Germany and the United States, we are still in the research stage, and few companies are involved in the subject. For example, the Mexican company Einnovación S.A. de C.V., together with the Center for Research and Technological Development and the Center for Advanced Technology Queretaro unit, developed a prototype of a hydrogen production system from water called Triton 50 (T50) for industrial applications.[166]

536. The approximate cost of green hydrogen, according to the International Energy Agency, is between USD 3 and USD 7 per kilo; this Agency calculates that, in the long term, in countries like Mexico and if solar panels are used for hydrogen production, the cost of hydrogen would be USD 1.6 to USD 2.2 per kilo.[167]

537. There is currently no constitutional or legislative framework in Mexico to regulate the use or exploitation of hydrogen as fuel. Hydrogen is not within the

166. *See*: https://centrosconacyt.mx/objeto/hidrogeno/.
167. *See*: https://www.forbes.com.mx/nuestra-revista-hidrogeno-verde-la-apuesta-energetica-en-mexico/.

description of natural resources or national goods indicated in Article 27 of the Political Constitution of the United Mexican States. But that does not mean that the door to creating a legal framework to regulate the use of hydrogen is completely closed. The paragraph 3 of Article 27 of the Constitution states: 'the nation shall at all times have the right to impose on private property the modalities dictated by the public interest, as well as that of regulating, for social benefit, the use of natural elements susceptible of appropriation.'

538. At the country's early stage of hydrogen utilization, current energy legislation covers the basics, including legislation such as that for natural gas storage and transportation. However, as this industry grows, legislation will need to be drafted. According to the National Electricity System Development Program 2020-2034, natural gas will continue to be predominant for electricity production, and clean energies will gradually incorporate.

§6. Bioenergetics

539. The backbone of Mexican biofuels legislation is the Law for the Promotion and Development of Bioenergy and its regulations, published in the Official Journal of the Federation in 2008 and 2009, respectively.

540. Article 2, section II of that Law defines bioenergetics as:

> II. Fuels obtained from biomass from organic matter from activities, agriculture, livestock, forestry, aquaculture, algaculture, fishing residues, domestic, commercial, industrial, microorganisms, and enzymes, as well as their derivatives, produced by processes sustainable technology that comply with the specifications and quality standards established by the competent authority in terms of this Law; taking into account the provisions of article 1, section I of this ordinance.

541. The Law refers specifically to bioenergetics produced from corn and designates Ministry of Agriculture and Rural Development as the competent authority to grant the corresponding permits in terms of section VIII of Article 11.

> VIII. Grant prior permits for producing bioenergetics from corn grain in its various modalities, which will be granted only when there are surplus inventories of internal corn production to satisfy national consumption.

542. In Mexico, the sale and use of biofuels, ethanol, and biodiesel are permitted when complying with permits and regulations; however, their production and consumption are generally limited.

543. The legislator tried to protect corn as a bioenergetic because it is a sensitive issue in Mexico; since being a country whose cultural roots are based on corn, it is worrying that today we have to import it.

544. Regarding other seeds, Article 12 of the Law mentions that SENER has the powers to: 'Grant and revoke permits for the production, storage, transportation and distribution through pipelines and the commercialization of bioenergetics.'

545. Article 18 considers that those contributing to the development and modernization of the bioenergy industry should receive incentives as well as those people who carry out technology research, the application of which reduces the generation of polluting emissions to the atmosphere, waters, soils, sites, as well as technological innovation in bioenergy production plants

546. Mexican Official Norm MON-016-CRE of 2016 prohibits the use of ethanol in gasoline sold in the metropolitan areas of the Valley of Mexico, Guadalajara and Monterrey; however, it allows a volume of 5.8% of anhydrous ethanol as an oxygenate in regular and premium gasoline in the rest of the national territory.

547. In 2017, the MON was modified in order to increase the maximum anhydrous ethanol content to 10% in gasoline in the rest of the national territory, but the ban was maintained in the metropolitan areas of the Valley of Mexico, Guadalajara and Monterrey.

548. In early 2020, the SCJN ruled that the 2017 modification to NOM-016-CRE was unconstitutional, since by:

> the magnitude of the damage to air quality that could be caused by the use of ethanol as an oxygenate in gasoline is under debate, the so-called 'environmental precautionary' principle is fully applicable, which requires an assessment to be carried out with as much scientific information as possible, regarding the potential damage that the increase in ethanol for these purposes could cause to the environment.

§7. The Role of Lithium

549. Lithium is a fundamental mineral for the storage of electricity. It is widely used in the manufacture of batteries. According to the constitution, it is considered national property, and, although ordinarily private individuals can exploit subsoil minerals by obtaining a concession, in 2022, the Congress of the Union approved a reform to the Mining Law to state in Article 5 Bis. the following:

> Article 5 Bis. Lithium is declared to be of public utility, so no concessions, licenses, contracts, permits or authorizations will be granted in this matter. Those areas with lithium deposits will be considered mining reserve zones.

It is recognized that lithium is the Nation's patrimony, and its exploration, exploitation, benefit and use are reserved in favour of the Mexican people.

The state will administer and control the economic value chains of lithium through the public agency mentioned in Article 10 of this Law.

The Mexican Geological Service will assist the decentralized public agency in charge of lithium's exploration, exploitation, benefit and use in the location and recognition of the geological areas in which there are probable lithium reserves.

In the exploration, exploitation, benefit and use of lithium and its value chains, it will be the duty of the Mexican State to protect and guarantee the health of Mexicans, the environment and the rights of native peoples, indigenous and Afro-Mexican communities.

Part VI. Interaction Between Energy Law and Environmental Law

Introduction

550. Given that, from exploration to final consumption, all activities associated with the energy sector imply considerable negative impacts on the environment, environmental implications must be discussed when analysing energy legislation.

551. For instance, electricity transmission lines or oil and gas pipelines are lineal facilities that could affect natural and sociocultural resources. The impacts of short lines are local, but the longest ones can produce regional results. Most of such effects occur on or near the right of way (ROW), that is to say, the area of land where the structures supporting the line are placed, including clearance allowances. The higher the voltage, the higher the impacts, and bigger support structures are required to increase the corresponding environmental impacts.[168] The same consideration is applicable to oil and gas pipelines.

552. The negative environmental effects of electricity transmission lines and pipelines are caused by their construction, operation, and maintenance. The leading causes of such impacts associated with this infrastructure include land clearing of the ROW, building access ways, and placement of towers and substations. In addition, maintenance work includes chemical or mechanical control of vegetation over the ROW. Finally, the impacts of transmission lines on the landscape are also considerable.

553. Environmental legislation addresses the control or mitigation of all transmission lines' negative impacts at the national level. However, in cases of regional markets, when environmental legislation is not homogeneous in all the countries, the apparent economic benefits of electricity exports may hide tremendous ecological impacts for the country where the electricity is produced or where the transmission networks are placed.[169]

---

168. There are currently three high-tension interconnections between the US and Mexico and several other transmission projects have been studied and proposed, particularly in the Arizona-Sonora corridor. *See* Edward A. Hoyt et al., 'Environmental Implications of Increased US-Mexico Electricity Trade' (1999), available at http://www.sciencedirect.com (accessed 25 Sep. 2011).
169. In 2002, the environmental groups Earth Justice and Wild Earth Advocates, representing the Border Power Plant Working Group, filed a lawsuit against the US government challenging permits

554. As mentioned before, nuclear energy has been considered clean energy with low environmental impacts in the same vein. However, the risk of catastrophic events associated with this energy source is enormous. Because of that building and operation of Laguna Verde nuclear plant in Mexico were conditioned to the approval of the Civil Liability for Nuclear Damages Act. This law channels civil liability to nuclear facilities operators when a nuclear accident is produced. However, the main weakness of this piece of legislation consists of the fact that it caps the maximum economic compensation that such an operator has to pay to restore the caused damage.

555. Thus, the holistic study of Energy Law must include two categories of regulations:

(1) *Sectoral laws.* The Mining Act,[170] HL, Law of the Electricity Industry (LEI), and Regulatory Act in Article 27 of the Constitution on Nuclear Matters.[171]
(2) *Environmental legislation.* The General Law constitutes the legislation related to the protection of the environment on Ecological Equilibrium and Environment Protection the National Waters Act; the General Act for Sustainable Use of Forest Act; the General Law of Wildlife Act, the General Law for Prevention and Comprehensive Management of Wastes, and the Federal Law of Environmental Liability, as well as regulations under such laws.

556. The sectorial legislation refers to the exploration and exploitation regime for the resources and, where this is allowed, granting concessions for private investments. These categories of laws have been already analysed in previous chapters of this monograph. Environmental legislation is discussed in this chapter.

---

granted to two companies planning to build electrical transmission lines from Baja, Mexico into California. The lines were built to take power from two electrical generation plants being built three miles inside of Mexico to supply power to the United States. The plaintiff held that 'Approving transmission lines for power plants under construction in Mexicali, without ensuring that these plants are built to minimize air and water quality impacts, will cause unnecessary harm to local US and Mexican communities.' *See* Earth Justice, 'Environmentalists Sue over Transmission Lines from Mexico to US', 19 Mar. 2002, available at http://earthjustice.org.

170. Published on 26 June 1996 reformed in 1996.
171. Published on 4 Dec. 1989.

Chapter 1. Enforcement and Compliance

557. Although the Federal Congress passed the first Mexican Environmental Law in 1971 and the first environmental agency was created in the same year, enforcement had been the Achilles' heel of environmental policy. However, the entry into the force of NAFTA in 1994 positively stimulated the environmental performance for Mexico.

558. It seems paradoxical, as energy sector legislation has changed to open several activities to private investors' participation during the past two decades. As a result of NAFTA signature, environmental laws and particularly their enforcement, have become stricter.

559. Barely had NAFTA negotiations been initiated that USA environmental groups voiced three concerns about the free trade area:[172]

(1) First, that NAFTA would encourage US businesses to move to Mexico to take advantage of lower environmental standards or lax enforcement.[173]
(2) Second, an FTA with Mexico would exacerbate the terrible environmental problems of the border region.
(3) Third, the FTA could be a way to challenge US environmental regulations.

560. That criticism provoked the following effects:

(1) NAFTA was 'greened' with several rules related to environmental protection.[174]
(2) The signature of NAFTA by Canada and the USA was conditioned to adopting a North American Side-Agreement on Environmental Cooperation (NAAEC).[175]

---

172. Mayer F, *Negotiating NAFTA: Political Lessons for the FTAA* (2001), available at www. pubpol.duke.edu.
173. Gallagher holds that 'Although the majority of firms that move to Mexico do not move there because of low environmental standards, this does not imply that when firms move to Mexico they are model environmental corporations. In fact, the World Bank conducted a survey of over 200 firms in Mexico and found that, contrary to prevailing assumptions, foreign firms were no more likely than domestic firms to comply with Mexican environmental law.' Gallagher K, *Free Trade and Environment: Mexico, NAFTA and Beyond* (2004).
174. Mol A, *Globalization and Environmental Reform: The Ecological Modernizations of the Global Economy* (2001).
175. In the words of Bailey, NAAEC 'was designed to assuage fears that Mexico would became a heaven for pollution once NAFTA took effect drawing all industry south the border where environmental enforcement was weak'. Bailey K, *Citizen Participation in Environmental Enforcement in Mexico and the United States: A Comparative Study* (Winter 2004) Georgetown International Environmental Law Review, available at http://findarticles.com. Trade officials from Canada, Mexico and the United States began negotiations in March 1993. On 14 Sep. 1993, the three countries concluded negotiations on environmental and labour side accords that include provisions to address problems with enforcement of environmental and labour laws.

(3) Mexico and USA adopted a plan to deal with environmental problems at the border.[176]
(4) The Mexican government created the Attorney General Office for Environmental Protection (AGOEP) as an administrative agency to improve Mexico's national strategy for environmental law enforcement.[177]
(5) The General Act for Ecological Balance and Environmental Protection (in Spanish LGEEPA) was amended for the first time, among other reasons to comply with commitments assumed by Mexico in both NAFTA and its Environmental Side-Agreement.[178]
(6) The Mexican government issued several standards to comply with NAFTA's requirements on regulatory harmonization.

561. In this context, the signature of the Environmental Side-Agreement to NAFTA[179] and NAAEC was to avoid the negative environmental impacts of international trade. In that sense, some of the most critical commitments assumed by signatory parties are:

(1) Each country shall ensure that its laws and regulations provide for high levels of environmental protection and shall strive to continue to improve those laws and regulations (Article 3).
(2) Each party shall effectively enforce its environmental laws and regulations through appropriate governmental action (Article 5).

562. When NAFTA negotiations started, Canada and the USA had already established agencies to enforce environmental regulations.[180] In 1992, Mexico's Government established the AGEP. AGEP was given the power to enforce environmental laws to deter foreign investors from seeing Mexico as a polluter's heaven. AGEP's creation represented an essential step in institutional harmonization required by the economic integration of the three countries. However, AGEP was not given faculty to enforce NWA, which is still reserved to NWC.

---

176. 'In separate negotiations, the United States and Mexico agreed to establish a Border Environmental Cooperation Commission (BECC) and a North American Development Bank (NAD Bank) to provide financing for environmental investments. NAFTA implementing legislation passed Congress in November, 1993, and the agreement entered into force on January 1, 1994.' Fletcher S & Tiemann M, *Trade and Environment: GATT and NAFTA* (Congressional Research Service, Library of Congress, 1994).
177. *See*: *Reglamento Interior de la Secretaría de Desarrollo Social*, Official Journal of the Federation 4 Jul. 1992 and *Acuerdo que regula la organización y funcionamiento interno del Instituto Nacional de Ecología y de la Procuraduría Federal de Protección al Ambiente*, Official Journal of the Federation 17 Jul. 1992.
178. Published in: Official Journal of the Federation 13 Dec. 1996.
179. Signed in 1993 and enforceable since 1994. The agreement creates a framework to better conserve, protect and enhance the North American environment through cooperation and effective enforcement of environmental laws. *See* www. Naaec.gc.ca.
180. *See*: Gonzalez JJ, (ed.), *La naturaleza jurídica de la evaluacióndel impacto ambiental. Análisis de Derecho Comparado* (2011).

563. The Constitutional Energy Reform of 2013 creates, besides AGEP, the NAISEPES as a news agency in charge of enforcing environmental laws, specifically in the hydrocarbons industry. However, AGEP keeps the power of enforcing environmental laws in the case of the electricity industry. Thus enforcement of environmental regulations is a task of the AGEP, NWC and NAISEPES.

Chapter 2. National Environmental Legislation

§1. Land Use and Environmental Impact Authorizations

564. Nowadays, environmental legislation obliges investors in the energy sector to meet a series of requirements. First, according to Article 28, paragraph II of the Environmental Act, all activities related to the energy sector are required to obtain an environmental impact authorization from the Ministry of the Environment following the corresponding environmental impact assessment.[181] The regulations on environmental impact assessment specifically include building and operating infrastructure for electricity transmission, oil pipelines, refining plants, exploration and exploitation activities, etc.[182]

565. Second, when any of described activities implies impacts to forestlands, Article 58 of the General Act for Sustainable Development of the Forest[183] requires obtaining prior authorization for land-use change. According to the mentioned provision, the Ministry of Environment could grant the land-use change only by exception. However, as previously mentioned, new energy sector laws recognize that using land for energy purposes has pre-eminence over any other use, even forest use. Finally, if those activities are located on agricultural lands, a land-use authorization has to be issued by local governments.[184]

566. Neither the environmental impact authorization nor the land-use change authorizations are easy to obtain. Commonly both involve very costly environmental studies and a complete revision by the competent authorities. Additionally, in several recent cases, relevant projects have confronted the opposition of environmental groups.[185] As a result, both private and public investors in the energy sector may face costly and lengthy litigation processes.[186]

---

181. In the USA, the issuance of a connection permit for export purposes requires consideration of: (a) the impact of the new transmission line on the reliability of US Electricity System, and (b) the environmental impact of the project. The procedure to obtain the EIA in the USA is quite different from the Mexican one. By contrast, in Guatemala there is no legal provision that specifically requires the environmental authorization of energy networks. *See*: Aguilar G, et al., *Evaluación del Impacto Ambiental Transfronteriza en CentroAmerica. Lineamientos Generales* (2006).
182. *See* Art. 5, subpara. K-III of Regulation under the Environmental Act on Environmental Impact Assessment.
183. Official Journal of the Federation 25 Feb. 2003.
184. According to Art. 35 of the General Act of Human Settlements, it corresponds to municipal governments to regulate land use in their territory.
185. In November 2003, the FCE had to modify the course of the transmission line Potrerillos-Aguascalientes-Potencia, in Guanajuato, to avoid environmental impacts on the natural protected area of the Silva's Dam given the strong opposition of the environmental groups which asserted that the transmission line could affect the wildlife living in that area.
186. For instance, the 'Accountability Counsel' filed complaints on 30 Nov. 2010 on behalf of the villages of Paso Canoa and Santa Ursula, and on 17 Jan. 2011 on behalf of the neighbouring indigenous community of Cerro de Oro. The complaints detail harm caused by the Overseas Private Investment Corporation (OPIC)-supported Cerro de Oro Hydroelectric Project. The project entails converting the Cerro de Oro reservoir into a hydropower project. The Council held that the complainants had not received information about the project, impacts on indigenous groups had not

567. In addition to the mentioned environmental authorizations, investors must buy or rent the land where the infrastructures are placed, i.e., the ROW.[187] The ROW can be established on private, public and ejidos or community lands.[188] This ROW may be obtained through three mechanisms: (1) an easement from the property owner, (2) a purchase and sale agreement with the property owner, and (3) a rent agreement with the property owner. In all these cases, according to Articles 1097, 2248 and 2398 of the Civil Federal Code, landowners, where the line is placed have the right to receive economic compensation.

568. Sometimes acquiring the ROW is not easy given that in almost all Mexican agricultural lands as well as in those owned by ejidos there are a number of conflicts over property rights, so the first problem consists of identifying who has the legal capacity to grant the easement or to sell or rent the land.[189] However, since the Civil Code does not establish any criteria to determine the value of the economic compensation for the easement, it has to be established by negotiation between the constructor and the landowner, landowners may demand a very high price for rent or sale.

569. One of the most controversial issues the Mexican energy reform attempts to solve is the conflict between landowner rights and subsoil exploitation. According to Mexican Constitution the nation owns certain natural resources placed into the subsurface, such as waters, minerals or hydrocarbons. However, the national property does not include the land where such resources are located. In consequence, it is frequently possible to see a conflict between landowner rights and those holding a concession to exploit natural resources into the subsurface. In the past, paying economic compensation to landowners solved these conflicts. In most cases, such payment was unfair or insufficient to compensate landowner losses due to the impossibility of using the land according to their interest.

570. Mexican Constitution and secondary legislation allow the State to expropriate lands to exploit natural resources into the subsoil. However, in many cases, social opposition makes it impossible to adopt such kinds of measures. Sometimes the opposition is based on unfair economic compensation, but others are also based on environmental and religious considerations. One of the most representative cases

---

been considered, and that there were insufficient plans to address and mitigate social and environmental impacts. Complainants also note problems with land acquisition and the lack of a required, local grievance mechanism. *See* www.accountabilitycounsel.org.

187. An electricity line right of way (ROW) is a strip of land that an electricity utility uses to construct, maintain, repair or replace an overhead or underground power line. The ROW allows the utility to provide clearance from trees, buildings and other structures that could interfere with the line installation, maintenance and operation.

188. The non-mandatory standard NRF-014-FCE issued in 2001 recommends the right of way is 52.48 ft wide.

189. About 55% of Mexico's land area is agricultural land. Nearly 94% of these lands belong to *ejidos* and *comunidades*. On *ejidos and comunidades,* disputes related to inheritance and parcel boundaries are common. As a result, normally it is not easy to identify who holds property rights of these lands. *See* USAID, 'Country Profile: Property Rights and Resource Governance, Mexico' (undated), available at http://usaidlandtenure.net.

in this regard is the strong opposition that President Vicente Fox confronted when trying to expropriate ejidal lands to enlarge facilities of Mexico City airport in 2001. In this case, expropriation decree issued by the Executive was cancelled because people took arms avoiding the authority to enforce this measure arguing economic compensation was unfair.

571. Other illustrative cases happened in *Real de Catorce*, *San Luis Potosi,* in the centre of the country. Federal Government had granted some mining concessions into an area known as *Wirikuta* that is a holly territory according to indigenous people. As a result, the government had to cancel such concessions. Finally, in the energy sector is possible to mention the case of *La Parota*, which involves a hydropower plant in Colima State, where landowners have been fighting against the construction of this plant in defence of their right to live in the place where they were born.

572. On this regard, transitional provision number 8 of the constitutional energy reform prescribes that 'due its strategic character, activities of exploration and extraction of oil and other hydrocarbons, as well as public service of transmission and distribution of electricity … are considered of social interest and of public order, in consequence, they have preference over any other use of the land, use of surface and of the subsurface of lands … ' A similar provision is in the repealed Regulatory Act of Article 27 in the Field of Petroleum of 1958 and in the past, it provoked a series of social conflicts.

573. The new law of hydrocarbons includes a specific chapter to regulate this issue. Despite the constitutional provision, HL states surface use has to be negotiated with landowners. On the contrary, the new HL substitutes the expropriation of lands for temporary occupation of lands. Unlike what happened in the case of expropriation, where landowners definitively lose their property, temporal occupation means that the state temporally takes private property.

§2. Pollution Control

574. Air pollution is also an important negative effect of a carbon base economy such as the Mexican one. Signature and ratification of Kyoto Protocol have stimulated a process of discussion of air pollution legislation. Many administrative bodies have been created better to organize the Mexican public policies in this regard. This section discusses about air pollution legal regimen in the specific case of pollution associated to energy sector.

I. Air Pollution and Climate Change

575. As is well known, industrialized countries are responsible for the majority of the historical and current CO_2 emissions. For instance, the United States of America, the EU countries and the members of the former Soviet Union, as well as some emergent Asian economies, produce 60% of greenhouse gases. As a result of the Kyoto Protocol, those countries have to seriously reduce greenhouse gas emissions during the period 2008–2012. For some, this means that Annex I countries of Kyoto Protocol have to reduce their productivity with the consequent economic loss. In fact, the flexible mechanisms included in the Protocol allow those countries to meet reduction targets without significantly reducing their industrial and commercial activities. They are, however, obliged to underwrite the cost of implementing carbon trade, joint implementation, or Clean Development Mechanisms (CDM) projects.[190] In particular, the CDM could generate a movement of investment from countries with reduction commitments to non-Annex I countries.[191] As a result, although Mexico did not commit to any reductions, at least for the initial phase of the Kyoto Protocol's implementation,[192] it may benefit from hosting CDM projects.[193]

576. In Mexico, combustion of fossil fuels to produce energy generates 61% of the country's total CO_2 emissions. The remainder of the CO_2 emissions comes from land-use change (14%), management of waste (10%), agriculture (8%), and industrial processes (7%). Thus, energy efficiency is one of the important Mexican strategies for climate change mitigation. Energy efficiency actions yielded a reduction of energy consumption of 12,558 GWh (equivalent to 10.2 Mt of CO_2) in 2009.[194]

577. Mexico is responsible for no more than 1.6% of the world's total fossil fuel-based carbon emissions, placing it thirteen in the rank of emitter countries.[195] However, because of its geographical conditions, Mexico is very vulnerable to climate

---

190. For instance, according to official reports, for Canada, the implementation of Kyoto mechanism in other countries could cost USD 1.8 billion per year. Canadian Government, 'The Cost of Bill C-288 to Canadian Families and Businesses', available at www.ec.gc.ca.
191. According to paragraph 2 of Art. 12 of the Kyoto Protocol, the purpose of the Clean Development Mechanism shall be to assist parties not included in Annex I in achieving sustainable development and in contributing to the ultimate objective of the Convention, as well as to assist parties included in Annex I in achieving compliance with their quantified emission limitation and reduction commitments under Art. 3. Jaume explains that the Clean Development Mechanism's adoption was the result of the proposal by Brazil regarding the establishment of a 'Clean Development Fund' and of the United States' interest of implicating developing countries in greenhouse gases abatement. Jaume S.E., *El cumplimientodel Protocolo de Kioto Sobre Cambio Climático* (2003)..
192. Article 10 of the Protocol just confirms the obligations contained in the Climate Change Convention.
193. As published by the UNFCCC Secretariat, Mexico has registered seventy-three CDM projects. CDM project are in the areas of waste management, disposal sites management and substitution of fossil fuels for renewable sources of energy.
194. Mexico Fourth National Communication to United Nations Framework Convention on Climate Change, available at http://unfccc.int/resource/docs/natc/mexnc4s.pdf.
195. *See* Mexican Special Programme for Climate Change 2009–2010, Official Journal of the Federation 28 Aug. 2009.

change.[196] Every State in the Mexican Federation is confronted with at least one considerable threat from climate change effects.[197]

578. According to the National Institute of Ecology,[198] there are ten especially vulnerable sectors, including agriculture,[199] health[200] and water.[201] Forty million Mexicans living in extreme poverty conditions are particularly vulnerable to climate change.[202] This applies mainly in the northern parts of the country, where water scarcity is a central issue, and in the southern parts of the country, where tropical storms cause extensive damage to crop and livestock production.

579. The Mexican environmental law system does not provide a sufficient foundation for an appropriate policy on climate change issues. In 2012, the Federal Congress passed the General Act for Climate Change.[203] Article 2 states the Act's objectives to be regulating greenhouse gas emissions to stabilize their concentrations at the atmosphere in a level that avoids dangerous anthropogenic interferences in the climatic system as well as to regulate actions for climate change mitigation and adaption. The Act creates the National Institute for Ecology and Climate Change, establishes the general criteria for policies on mitigation and adaption, the national system for climate change and the instruments of this system.

580. In order to create a national system for climate change, the Act establishes an Inter-ministerial Commission of Climate Change and a Council for Climate Change[204] that is in charge of formulating and implementing national climate change policy,[205] as well as a Climate Change Council that function as a consultative and evaluative institution and comprise members representing civil society, private corporations and academic organizations. Among the instruments for climate change mitigation and adaptation, the Act establishes the climate change found, the

196. Adrian Fernández et al., 'Cambio Climatico y Acciones para enfrentarlo', in *Temas Selectos de Medio Ambiente*, ed. Ninfa Salinas Sada & Yolanda Alaniz (Mexico: Cámara de Diputados, 2011), 121–180.
197. Mexico is among the countries with high vulnerability because 15% of its national territory, 68% of its population and 71% of its GDP are highly exposed to risk of adverse direct impacts of climate change.
198. *See* the website of the National Institute of Ecology, available at www2.ine.gob.mx/ cclimatico/ edo_sector/sector/sector.html.
199. It is expected that, by 2030, over-exploitation and pollution of aquifers will make all irrigation districts economically unsustainable and that, by 2050, there will be a reduction of 5%–29% in the ability of the soil to produce corn and other cereals.
200. The risk of death from heat impacts will increase during the following years and some areas will be more vulnerable to diseases such as dengue or paludism as well as gastrointestinal infections. The effects will mostly be borne by children and old people.
201. From 2020 to 2050, the medium summertime temperature will increase by between 1°C and 3°C, and precipitation will decrease 5%–10% annually, diminishing the availability of water.
202. According to official data, the areas most vulnerable to climate change are the states of Baja California, Sonora and Sinaloa, the basin of the 'Rio Lerma' and the south of the country.
203. Official Journal of the Federation 6 Jun. 2012.
204. According to the Bill, this Commission will replace the Commission on Climate Change created in 2005.
205. Currently such functions are for the Inter-ministerial Commission on Climate Change (IMCCC).

register of emissions, environmental standards and the economic instruments. However, the Act is a very programmatic piece of legislation and does not modify the legal frame currently in force regarding to climate change which have been introduced in 1988 by the Environmental Act.

581. A number of legislative steps have also been taken at the State levels. In November 2010, the State of Veracruz passed the Act of Mitigation and Adaptation of Climate Change Effects.[206] In December 2010, the State of Chiapas[207] and the Federal district of Mexico City[208] both passed acts for climate change adaptation. Similar to the Federal Climate Change Act Bill, these new State acts create public institutions in charge of climate change policy and green funds to support such policies.

582. Climate change is still addressed by using just the traditional legal instruments provided by the Mexican Environmental Act. In this regard, neither the Environmental Act nor its regulation on air pollution consider any obligations of pollutant emissions reduction but to control them and many duties of informing about the quality and quantity of pollutants emitted by industrial activities.

583. The primary obligations imposed by Environmental Act to air polluters are:

(1) to obtain the licence of operation from MENR; and
(2) to meet the caps of emission established by environmental standards.

II. Soil and Water Pollution

584. The energy sector, specifically oil industry, is an essential source of soil and water pollution (continental and marine).

585. Soil pollution is an issue that traditionally has been approached by regulating waste management. In the case of the energy sector, inappropriate disposal of hazardous waste is the main cause of soil pollution. To control soil pollution, the General Act of Prevention and Integral Management of Waste was passed in 2003.[209]

586. Regarding soil pollution, two environmental standards have been issued:

206. Available at http://www.legisver.gob.mx/leyes/LeyesPDF/CLIMATICO020713.pdf.
207. Available at http://www.congresochiapas.gob.mx/index.php/Legislacion-Vigente/ley-para-la-adaptaci-n-y-mitigaci-n-ante-el-cambio-clim-tico-en-el-estado-de-chiapas.html.
208. Available at www.partidoverde.org.mx/pvem/2010/11/ley-de-cambio-climatico-del-df-ejemplo-para-ejecutivo-federal/.
209. Official Journal of the Federation 8 Oct. 2003.

(1) NOM-138-SEMARNAT/SS-2003, Maximum permissible limits of hydrocarbons in soil and specifications for its characterization and recovery.[210]
(2) NOM-147-SEMARNAT/SSA1-2004, Establishing criteria to define concentrations of remediation of soils polluted by arsenic, barium, beryllium, cadmium, chromo hexavalent, mercury, nickel, silver, lead, selenium, thallium, and/or vanadium.[211]

587. National Waters Act, General Act Environmental Balance and Environmental Protection and the Regulation under the Law of the Sea govern water pollution. Basically, these laws try to control water pollution by requiring a discharge permit to all pollutant sources. This permit is necessary to discharge residual waters in any national water body, including rivers, lagoons, or sea. Environmental standards set up the maximum limits of pollutants that polluters are allowed to discharge into national waters.

588. Activities of exploration and exploitation of hydrocarbons could also cause serious damage to water ecosystems as it happened in the Ixtoc wheel oil that blasted in 1979 in the Gulf of Mexico. International treaties regulate these issues.

589. Few national laws have incorporated the content of international treaties in relation to liability for environmental damages into national legal regimen.

III. Environmental Liability

A. Background

590. The civil liability regime could remedy damage caused to people or the environment and resulting from emissions generated by activities associated with the oil industry.

591. Mexican private law recognizes two types of liability: fault liability and strict liability. Fault liability is based on three elements: damage, fault (improper behaviour), and causation between that conduct and the harm. Strict liability does not require proof of fault. Because strict liability is linked to dangerous activities, i.e., those involving a considerable level of risk, it can be applied to environmental, and therefore climate change, damages.

592. Most Mexican environmental laws envisage the application of civil liability to remedy environmental damages. For instance, Article 203 of the Environmental Act (as amended in 1996) asserts that all persons contaminating or deteriorating the environment or affecting natural resources shall be responsible and forced to repair the resultant damage according to the Civil Code.

210. Official Journal of the Federation 29 Mar. 2005.
211. Official Journal of the Federation 2 Apr. 2007.

593. Similarly, Article 96*bis*-1 of the Waters Act provides that individuals or corporations that illegally discharge waste waters that cause contamination in a receiving body shall assume the responsibility of repairing the environmental damage caused.

594. According to Article 1915 of the Federal Civil Code, restoration of damage could consist of the re-establishment of the previous conditions or, when re-establishment is impossible, the payment of an economic compensation. However, Mexican environmental laws stress the priority of remediation over monetary compensation. For instance, Article 152*bis* of the Environmental Act (as amended in 1996) provides:

> When generation, the management or final disposition of dangerous waste or materials results in soil pollution, those responsible for the operation will carry out the necessary actions to recover and to re-establish the conditions of the soil, so as it can be designated to some of the activities foreseen in the applicable programme of urban development plans or of ecological zoning plans for such soil or area.

595. Article 10 of the Federal Environmental Liability Act establishes that any individual or legal entity that through its action or omission directly or indirectly causes damage to the environment will be liable and will be obligated to repair the damage, or, when repair is not possible, to make the appropriate environmental compensation, in accordance with the terms of this Act. In the same way, it will be obliged to carry out the necessary actions to avoid increasing the damage caused to the environment.

596. In contrast, Article 136 of the Forest Act prioritizes the payment of economic compensation over ecological restoration. In cases of damage caused to forest resources, the environment, ecosystems, or their components, the responsible party must provide the corresponding compensation.

597. Although the Waste Act does not establish the obligation to repair environmental damage, it allows for the restoration of soils polluted by hazardous wastes in Articles 78 and 79, which respectively provide:

> Article 78. In coordination with the Secretary of Health, the Secretary shall issue the MONs for the characterization of polluted places and shall evaluate the risks to the environment and public health that derive from them to determine, in function of the risk the restoration actions that proceed.
>
> Article 79. The regulation on land use and the programmes of ecological classification and of urban development shall be considered when determining the level of remediation of polluted places with hazardous waste, based on the risks that will be avoided.

598. In 2013, the *Federal Environmental Liability Act* was passed. According to Article 1, this law regulates liability that arises from damage to the environment. The new law obliges those causing environmental damages to restore when it is impossible to pay monetary compensation. However, this law regulates environmental liability only in the following cases:

(1) when restoration or compensation are required by filing any collective actions established in Article 17 of the Constitution;
(2) when restoration or compensation is required through the alternative dispute resolution mechanisms regulated by the law; or
(3) when environmental damages result from a criminal behaviour.

599. Article 4 of this law recognizes that environmental damage is different from civil damage caused to owners of natural resources. The Civil Codes govern this type of damage. *The Federal Environmental Liability Act* also points out that environmental liability is different from administrative and criminal responsibility. *The Federal Environmental Liability Act* is comprised of fifty-six provisions organized into three sections. The first section refers to environmental liability and includes three chapters that govern issues such as: defining the scope of the concept of environmental damage; legal consequences of environmental damage; restoration of environmental damage; judicial procedure to channel environmental liability, including legal standing, precautionary measures, burden of proof and scope of the ruling. This section also creates an Environmental Fund for Restoration. In general, this section introduces a series of modifications to traditional civil liability principles providing for restoration of and compensation for environmental damage. The second section governs alternative mechanisms for conflict resolution whereas the third section contains provisions intended to complement criminal liability. According to this new law, administrative responsibility is a matter of other environmental general laws. However, *the Federal Environmental Liability Act* includes a few provisions that complement regulation of economic fines (provided by other environmental laws such as the *General Act of Ecological Balance* and *Environmental Protection or the General Act of Wild Life*).

600. The analysis of *the Federal Environmental Liability Act* shows that there are many reasons to consider it a regressive law. For instance, it defines environmental damage in Article 20, section III as follows:

> An adverse and measurable loss, change, detriment, reduction, affectation or modification of a) habitats, b) ecosystems, or c) natural elements and resources and their chemical, physical or biological conditions, interactions among them and the environmental services they provide.

601. However, this concept is not so straightforward given that it does not clarify at which point the adverse change, detriment, reduction, affectation or modification becomes damage. The lack of certainty in this regard could make it difficult to enforce the provisions of the Act.

602. According to the Constitution, environmental law is ruled by the principle of shared jurisdictions, but in spite of this, the new *Liability Act* is a Federal Law. This means that local governments are not permitted to pass local laws regarding this matter, and in consequence, the new law could produce results contrary to the Federal Constitution. The comparative analysis of environmental liability regimes in other jurisdictions shows a trend of fashioning environmental liability as strict liability. However, *the Federal Environmental Liability Act* states in Article 11 that 'Liability for environmental damage shall not be a strict liability and it arises from illegal acts or omissions with the exemptions established by this Title.' However, notwithstanding this assertion, the Act then establishes five exemptions under Article 12:

(1) environmental liability will be strict when the damage directly or indirectly arises from;
(2) *any action or omission related to hazardous materials or wastes;*
(3) *use and operation of ships in coral reefs;*
(4) *the undertaking of hazardous activities; and*
(5) *in cases or conduct mentioned by Article 1913 of the Federal Civil Code.*

603. The objective of Article 12 is somewhat unclear. In the first instance, it seems like sections I, II and III aim to limit those cases where environmental liability is considered strict. Nevertheless, *the Federal Liability Act* excludes from the principle of non-strict liability those cases established in Article 1913 of *the Federal Civil Code*. This provision holds that:

> Those persons using mechanisms, instruments, devices or substances that are dangerous because of the speed they develop, its explosive or inflammable nature, the energy of power they transmit or analogous causes, are liable for the damage caused even when they do not act illegally except where they demonstrate that the damages is a result of the negligence of the victim.

604. The analysis of the above provision shows that it includes all the cases mentioned by paragraphs I, II and II of Article 12 of the *Liability Act* and many others because the scope of Article 1913 of *the Federal Civil Code* is very wide. It is reasonable to conclude that according to the new *Liability Act*, environmental liability lacks clarity.

605. Similarly, whereas modern liability regimes around the world have inverted the burden of proof in order to promote environmental justice, Article 36 of *the Federal Liability Act* holds that:

> The link of causation between the damage and the conduct attributed to the defendant must be proven in the trial proceedings.

606. *The Federal Environmental Liability Act* gives priority to restoration over economic compensation. Article 13 holds in that regard that restoration of environmental damage will consist of rehabilitating habitats, ecosystems, natural elements and resources to their base line chemical, physical or biological conditions as well as the relationships among them and the environmental services they provide. However, this law does not define any criteria to determine when the damaged environment has been restored.

607. According to Article 14, economic compensation is allowed when the restoration is material or technically impossible, which is coherent with the trend shown by comparative environmental law. However, this provision adds several cases where restoration can be substituted by economic compensation, which is not straightforward. The cases are described by section II of Article 14, which holds that damage resulting from activities conducted without having environmental impact authorization or without having land-use change authorization can be compensated to obtain such authorizations. This is another reason to conclude that the Federal *Environmental Liability Act* is regressive.

608. The Federal Environmental Liability Act does not modify the Federal Code of Civil Procedure provisions regarding the scope of the ruling.

609. Finally, Mexico is missing a regulation on the transboundary environmental impact of both:

(1) regional networks of electricity transmission, pipelines or any other infrastructure; and
(2) energy plants that generate electricity or refine oil to be transported and distributed beyond the country's frontiers where such facilities are placed.[212]

This gap in the legislation prevents adequate and complete evaluation of the environmental impacts resulting from Mexico's integration with both North and Central American electricity markets.

IV. Social Liability

610. The objective of the energy reform is twofold: on the one hand, to give legal certainty to private investment with the guarantee that host communities, landowners or non-governmental organizations would not oppose the energy project,

212. In fact, the original plan Puebla Panamá contemplated a number of environmental strategies to be implemented alongside the regional development plans such as the harmonization of environmental impact assessment systems across Central American countries. However, such strategies have not been implemented yet. Comisión Centroamericana de Ambiente y Desarrollo, 'Transversalidad del tema ambiental en el Plan Puebla Panamá- Analisis y recomendaciones' (2004), available at www.ccad.ws.

and on the other hand, to make these actors feel that they are part of the decision-making process and that they will benefit from the energy project.

611. Thus, Article 25 of the Constitution establishes that:

> under criteria of social equity, productivity and sustainability, companies in the social and private sectors of the economy shall be supported and promoted, holding them to the modalities dictated by public interest and the use, in general benefit, of productive resources taking care of their conservation and the environment.

612. Articles 118 of the Law of Hydrocarbons (HL) and 117 of the LEI state that public and private infrastructure projects of the hydrocarbon and electricity industries must take into account the principles of sustainability and respect for human rights of those communities and towns of the areas in which they intend to develop.

613. The energy reform introduced a few new legal instruments aimed at evaluating the social impacts of energy sector activities and compel private companies to assume social and environmental liabilities, protect the right to a healthy environment, and achieve sustainable development of the energy sector.

614. The new instruments are:

- the social licence;
- the social impact assessment;
- benefit-sharing with affected communities; and
- host communities' participation in the benefits.

A. The Social Licence

615. As Don Smith states, social licence is an 'ongoing social contract with society that allows a project to both start and continue operating in a community'.[213] In Mexico, the approval of a project by the host community became a requirement to comply within 2001, after an indigenous community that owned the land where a new airport for Mexico City was to be built blocked it by force.[214] Although, at the

213. Don C. Smith, *Social Licence to Operate in the Unconventional Oil and Gas Development Sector. The Colorado Experience*, in *Sharing the Costs and Benefits of Energy and Resource Activity. Legal Change and Impact on Communities* 123 (Lila Barrera-Hernández Lila Barrera et.al. ed. UK Oxford University Press 2016).

214. In 2001, the former President of Mexico Vicente Fox Quezada issued an Executive Decree for expropriation of indigenous lands in Texcoco, State of Mexico that provoked a mobilization by indigenous peasants against the project. J. Carlos Dominguez, 'Discourses and Conditions of Possibility in Latin American Social Movements: The Cases of the Bolivian "Water War" and the Movement of Opposition Against the New Airport in Mexico City' *QEH Working Paper Series—QEHWPS171*, October 2008, available at http://www3.qeh.ox.ac.uk.

time, the requirement of a social licence did not have a basis in the law, it became increasingly common for companies to negotiate with the host community or the directly affected landowners for the approval of a project. On the contrary, an increase in social opposition to energy projects was observed. The more vulnerable to a project the community may be, the stronger the potential opposition. The participation of private companies in the energy sector required some level of assurance that community opposition would not be an obstacle to development. To achieve this, it was necessary to legalize the procedure whereby a social licence may be issued. Accordingly, Articles 199 of HL and 118 of EIL state that the ME shall:

- conduct a public consultation; and
- inform contractors or assignees of the presence of vulnerable social groups in those areas where activities under assignments and contracts will be carried out for the necessary actions to be implemented to safeguard a community's rights.

616. In addition, under Articles 120 of HL and 119 of LEI, to take into account the interests and rights of communities and indigenous peoples, the ME is required to conduct free, prior, and informed consultation, as well as any other information processes that are necessary for safeguarding such interests and rights. According to Articles 85 of the Regulation under HL and 89 of the Regulation under EIL when Productive State Corporations develop the projects, prior consultation procedures shall be conducted by such enterprises. In the consultation procedures, the ME may provide for the participation of the National Security Agency for Industrial and Environmental Protection of the Hydrocarbons Sector, Productive State Corporations (PEMEX and FCE) and their subsidiaries and affiliates, as well as individuals, by applicable regulations. As required by Article 120 of HL, the consultation procedures shall aim to reach an agreement or, where appropriate, social consent. Unfortunately, EIL does not recognize this last objective. Consequently, for electricity projects, the requirement of public consultation does not imply that a social licence is required.

617. In principle, the social licence is only required for new hydrocarbon projects and not for already underway ones.

B. Social Impact Assessment

618. The new energy laws refer to social impact assessment in two ways. First, Article 199 of the HL establishes that, prior to granting any assignation or bid publication for an exploration and exploitation contract, the ME, in coordination with the Ministry of the Interior and other competent authorities, shall conduct a Social Impact Study of the relevant area, this study has not authorizing purposes, it is only an instrument for the decision-making process. The results of the study must be made available to the entitlement holder, once the allocation has been granted, or provided to bid participants.[215]An assignment may not be granted or a call for bid for an Exploitation and Exploitation Contract may not be published without the study referred to above. The EIL does not include a similar provision. The Social Impact Study shall contain:

(a) A socio-demographic characterization of the areas and regions where they are located.
(b) Identification of vulnerable groups.
(c) A description of the legal status of the land where the project will be carried out.
(d) Preliminary estimation of social impacts.

619. Second, both the HL, in Article 121, and the LEI, in Article 120, refer to the obligation of assignees and contractors to conduct social impact assessments.

620. Accordingly, those interested in obtaining permits or authorizations to develop energy sector projects shall submit a social impact assessment to the ME. This document must contain the identification, characterization, and assessment of the social impacts that might arise from their activities and mitigation measures and corresponding social management plans, in the terms established by the Regulations under EIL and HL.[216] Article 79 of the Regulation of the HL dictates 'those interested in obtaining a permit to develop projects in the Hydrocarbon Industry shall submit to the ME the Social Impact Assessment referred to in the Law'. In contrast, according to the mentioned provision, 'Those interested in obtaining a permit to carry out commercialization activities of Hydrocarbons, Petroleum and Petrochemicals shall not be subject to the obligation established by this article, given that they do not carry out works or infrastructure development.'

C. Sharing Benefits with the Community

621. The Mexican Constitution and secondary legislation refer to different types of 'community'. First, the Mexican Constitution refers to the Mexican people as holder of national sovereignty represented by the Mexican State. The Mexican Constitution vests the property of hydrocarbons and other natural resources in the nation; thus, it corresponds to all Mexicans as a community represented by the government to decide on the exploitation of such resources.

622. Second, Article 27 of the Constitution refers to indigenous communities that, as Barton and Goldsmith assert, 'live on the land, live off the land, and identify with it spiritually'.[217] Section VII of Article 27 of the Constitution holds: 'The

215. Mayer-Brown, *Analysis of Mexico's New Hydrocarbons Legal Regime* (2014), available at https://www.mayerbrown.com/files/Publication.
216. In the case of the HL, the social impact assessment also has to include social management plans.
217. *See* chapter by Barton and Goldsmith in this book. Rehacer referencia.

legal capacity of *ejidos*[218] and communal population centres is recognized and their ownership over the land is protected, whether for human settlements as well as for productive activities.'[219]

623. The constitutional protection granted to indigenous peoples is crucial because it is common for energy projects to disturb the relation between the indigenous communities and the land targeted for development. Frequently, the development of energy projects results in displacement to places they do not feel connected. The annoyance is more significant when communities know that these projects generate enormous profits that will not be shared with them.

624. The Environmental Act refers to 'community' as the group of people, not necessarily indigenous, that can be affected by an energy project and so have a legal interest and empowers that group to challenge the authorization of the project. The link among this group of persons is not the land but their human right to a healthy environment.

625. Finally, the Federal Code of Civil Procedures refers to 'community' as a group of people that is able to seek damages when a right they have in common is affected.

626. Landowners are not necessarily a fixed community, but when their individual interests are affected by the same cause, they often form territorially defined communities[220] that unite to defend their environmental and/or civil rights against energy projects that affect those individual rights. Based on the Environmental Act and the Federal Code of Civil Procedures, these territorially defined communities have legal standing to file different actions against a project, including actions for environmental damages.

627. Opening the energy sector may mean the multiplication of cases of conflict between assignees and contractors on the one hand and, on the other, indigenous communities, affected persons, and landowners. This means that the Mexican State, as the owner of hydrocarbon resources, and also in its role as protector of those natural resources affected by energy sector projects, should prevent the generation of negative social and environmental impacts and ensure that a portion of profits generated by energy projects is directed to national development in general and, in particular, to compensate the impacts on communities (including indigenous peoples) and landowners.

628. In that context, the energy reform introduced three mechanisms that force energy companies to share their profits with the community at three levels:

---

218. An *ejido* is an area of communal land used for agriculture on which community members individually possess and farm a specific parcel.
219. Mexican Supreme Court, Political Constitution of Mexican United States (2008) available at https://www.scjn.gob.mx/leyes/Documents/Political_Mexican_States_2008.pdf.
220. Barton B, et.al. *Community and Sharing*, in *Sharing the Costs and Benefits of Energy and Resource Activity* (Lilia Barrera-Hernández et.al. ed., Oxford University Press 2016).

(1) all Mexicans as represented by the Mexican State;
(2) host communities; and
(3) directly affected landowners.

629. The next sections analyse each one of the mechanisms mentioned above.

630. The HL addresses this issue very lightly by noting in the last paragraph of Article 120:

> The Ministry of Energy, with the opinion of the Ministry of Finance, may include in the Assignments, as well as the terms and conditions established for the bidding process, the amounts and rules for determinations of the amount that Contractor or Assignee must allocate for the sustainable and human development of the communities in which the activities are to be carried out, in health, education, family, and labor development matters, among others.

631. According to the cited provision, the ME has the power to define the amounts that have to be set aside for sustainable and human development of host communities; it is reasonable to expect that during the process of consultation, the community will have an opportunity to influence the ministry's decision.

D. The Land-Use Compensation

632. In Mexico, private property, as well as indigenous community's lands, are subject to those faculties that Article 27 of the Constitution grants to the Nation with the aims of:

- To expropriate it, temporarily occupy it and impose it those limitations as demanded by the public interest.
- *To impose property those modalities as dictated by the social interest, this faculty includes the possibility of establishing specific land uses.*

633. Under the mentioned constitutional basis, Article 71 of EIL points out two principles in which property right can be affected by the Energy Industry activities, these principles are:

(1) Given that electricity industry is considered a public utility, it proceeds the superficial taking or affectation or the establishment of necessary servitudes to provide the public service of transmission and distribution of energy, and to build generation plants in those cases in which, due to the characteristics of the project, a specific location is required.
(2) Transmission and distribution of electricity activities are considered as of social interest and public order, and so such activities have priority over any other that implies the use of the surface and subsurface of the lands affected by them.

634. On the other side, Article 96 of HL sets up similar rules by saying:

- Hydrocarbons industry is considered a public utility and so it precedes the establishment of the necessary servitudes, superficial taking or affectations to conduct its activities.
- Exploration and Exploitation activities are considered a social interest and public order and so they have priority over any other that implies the use of the surface and subsurface of the lands affected by them.

635. In consequence, the enforcement of the mentioned provisions could result in a conflict between the land owner interest in using the land and the holder of a permit who pretends to carry out any hydrocarbons or electricity industries activities.

636. For instance, based on the public interest, historically, PEMEX has taken unfair advantage of landowners, paying ridiculous amounts of money for the temporary or permanent occupation of the land where projects were located.

637. In the past, PEMEX and the Mexican State did not share the benefits generated by their projects with host communities or landowners. The same happened in the case of electricity projects.

638. The new energy laws strive to reverse this trend. Even when pursuant to Article 71 of the Electricity Act (2013), transmission and distribution of electricity have special priority over any other activities that involve the use of the surface and subsurface of lands lying within the limits of the respective projects. Article 73 adds that the consideration for the purchase, use, or occupation of land, goods, or rights that are necessary for conducting these activities shall initially be negotiated directly between the interested parties. Should they not come to agreement, the industry participant may request that: (i) a district judge granted a legal easement, or (ii) the Ministry of Agricultural, Territorial and Urban Development conduct mediation. Lack of agreement after the mediation may also result in the imposition of a legal easement (Article 79). The State determines the compensation for mandatory easements and, in most cases, turns out to be unfair.

639. The new Law of Hydrocarbons (2014) also deals with this issue. Article 100 provides that economic compensation; the terms and conditions for the use, possession, or encumbrance of land; and property and rights needed to perform activities of exploration and exploitation of hydrocarbons shall be negotiated and agreed between the owners, possessors, or holders of such land, property, or rights, and assignees or contractors. However, two differences with electricity can be found. First, the Law of Hydrocarbons does not establish the rule of preferential use of land for hydrocarbon projects. Second, Article 100 provides that acquisition of lands for those purposes is allowed only in cases of private property, but in the case of *ejidos* and communal property only temporary occupation is allowed.

Part VII. Conclusions

640. The analysis conducted in this monograph allows pointing out a number of conclusions that resumes the state of the art of Mexican Energy Sector Law and it's environmental implications and stresses the imperative of modifying the public policies in this regard:

(1) Contrary to what is generally assumed, the original text of the Mexican Constitution did not establish the model of absolute property of the State over hydrocarbon resources. The principles governing hydrocarbons property and exploitation are the result of a process of constitutional reforms aimed at establishing the sovereignty of the Mexican nation over hydrocarbons and other natural resources. However, this process had not yet concluded when the secondary legislation started turning back the privatization of the energy sector. Private investment in oil industry has been a constant in Mexican economy. All the indicators suggest that the process of privatization will continue during the following years even without modifying the Constitution, which appears to be unnecessary.
(2) Despite the constitutional provisions, as a consequence of a series of legal and regulatory reforms passed during and after NAFTA negotiations, during the years before 2013, private investment was already allowed to participate in generation of electricity as well as in transmission infrastructure. By the last decade of the twentieth century, the Mexican electricity sector has already passed from an absolute monopoly of the State to a single buyer model.
(3) By that time, Mexico's energy legislation allowed participation of private investors in building and operating electricity infrastructure. However, private electricity networks had a limited objective. Private networks were only allowed to be built for import and export purposes. In addition, there were many disincentives to private investment in energy networks.
(4) When NAFTA went into force and Mexican Energy Law was consequently amended to allow private investment in energy networks, the national energy transmission system under the control of FCE had already covered almost the entire Mexican territory.
(5) Whereas the Electricity for Public Service Law allowed importers and exporters to transmit electricity through the national energy system owned by FCE, building their own electricity networks could represent a number of problems to private investors such as conflicts with environmental groups or difficulties in obtaining the required authorizations.

(6) In sum, private investors did not have real incentives to build or operate their own electricity networks. Although a few permits for exporting energy had been granted to independent producers in the north of the country, producers preferred to be connected to national energy network. As a result, FCE operates as the single buyer and distributor of electricity while private investment focuses more on electricity generation than on electricity transmission.

(7) Thus, even when private networks were permitted by Mexican legislation, investing in this area resulted unattractive. Consequently, the Mexican electricity model has passed from a full State monopoly model to a state monopoly model on transmission and distribution of electricity.

(8) Mexico's energy integration with the North and with the South has different characteristics. In the case of the Mexico-US energy market, when international trade took off, each country already had a developed national network. In the Mexico-Guatemala case, it was necessary to build electricity infrastructure to send electricity to that country but because of the limitations on the Mexican side no private investment participated in building this infrastructure. However, neither the integration process with the North American Market nor Mexico's participation in the Central American electricity networks has substantially influenced the development of the national electricity system.

(9) So far, a number of plans, programmes, laws, regulations, and standards have been enacted by Mexico in the field of environmental protection and energy exploitation. Although such documents refer indirectly to the problems analysed in this monograph, they do not reflect the existence of a real policy regarding renewable energies. Moreover, most of the existing legal and administrative instruments' references to the issues under analysis are disconnected and sometimes contradictory. This can be explained by the fact that planning in Mexico is based on methodologies that only take into account the short-term economic cost of energy generation. The lack of consideration of the benefits that may derive from renewable energy for the national economy, such as long-term price stability and risk reduction in relation to supply, together with the fact that Mexico has important fossil energy resources, explain why national energy policies and scenarios continue to rely on fossil fuels.

(10) Despite the enormous possibilities that Mexico has to introduce environmentally friendly sources of energy, it depends mainly on the oil industry. As a result, the Mexican economy is very vulnerable to any international fossil fuel market changes. At the same time, Mexican demand for energy continues to increase. Mexico needs to establish a comprehensive energy policy to satisfy the local energy demand and reduce its dependence on oil exports. In addition, the Mexican government needs to deal with the environmental impacts caused by the production, transportation and consumption of fossil fuels.

(11) Apparently, Mexican Constitutional Energy Reform of 2013 is simple. It is simple because it introduces into the Mexican Constitution a few new rules. The reform consisted of introducing into the Constitution words that in the

past had been deleted from the constitutional text whereas in other cases, the amendment deleted from the Constitution words that in the past had been incorporated into it.

(12) In this way, a confrontation of the constitutional text as amended with the original one established by the 1940s reform shows that Peña Nieto's government position in regard to energy sector is as nationalist as President Cardenas' expropriation Decree of 1938.

(13) Despite the aforementioned, Mexican Constitutional Energy Reform is complex because it does not only consist of those changes incorporated to Articles 25, 17, and 28 of the Constitution's Transitory provisions of the amendment introduced as well other important rules.

(14) The twenty-one transitional provisions make private investment possible in the Mexican energy sector, create new regulatory agencies, and establish financial mechanisms and institutions to use revenues from this sector to push long-term national development.

(15) In consequence, the Mexican Constitutional Energy Reform is also fundamental because it constitutes the last stage of an opening process in a sector of the Mexican economy that could not continue monopolized by the State.

(16) Even when the Congress passed secondary legislation implementing new constitutional framework, new energy laws were not necessary. When the Mexican Federal Congress passed new nine laws and reformed other eleven legal bodies, transitional provisions had already opened the Mexican energy sector.

Selected Bibliography

Adrian, L. *El gobierno de la industria petrolera Mexicana.* 2007, available at siteresources.worldbank.org, 37.

Aguayo, S. *El almanaque mexicano.* 2007.

Bazán-Perkins, S. *La energía nuclear: una alternativa de sustentabilidad para resolverla demanda eléctrica en México.* 2005, VI.3, 187.

Brañes, R. *Manual de Derecho Ambiental Mexicano.* México: Fondo de Cultura Económica, 1996.

Cárdenas, J. *Constitución y normas en materia petrolera, 2008*, available at http://www.redalyc.org/pdf/427/42723039009.pdf>.

Cardona Lara, M. 'La industria petrolera ante la regulación ecológica en México'. In *La industria petrolera ante la regulación jurídico- ecológica en México.* 1992.

Cienfuentes López, M. & Cienfuentes López, S.. 'El derecho constitucional a un medio ambiente adecuado en México'. *En Revista Mexicana de Legislación Ambiental, publicación revista cuatrimestral septiembre-diciembre.* año2, número 4. (2000): 55–63.

Comisión de Cooperación Ambiental para América del Norte. *Emisiones atmosféricas de las centrales eléctricas en América del Norte.* 2004, available at www.cec.org>.

'Climate Change Plan of 2005', available at www.climatechangeconnection.org>.

Díaz, M. 'El régimen jurídico ambiental del subsuelo en México'. In *PEMEX, ambiente y energía. Los retos del futuro*, edited by C. Cardona. 1995.

De Desarrollo, Plan Nacional. 2007–2012, sección economía competitiva y generadora de empleos: energía, electricidad e hidrocarburos, available at pnd.calderon-.presidencia.gob.mx.

De la Garza J. Ma., Serna. 'El régimen constitucional de la propiedad en México'. In *Derecho comparado Asia-México. Culturas y sistemas jurídicos comparados.* 2007.

Energy Information Agency (USA). *México: Country Analysis Brief.* 2003, available at www.eia.doe.gov. *See also* Petróleos Mexicanos (PEMEX). Reservas de Hidrocarburos en México 19 (2002).

Mar Campins, E. *Los retos de la aplicación del protocolo de Kyoto en España y Canadá.* Editorial Atelier, Protocolo de Kyoto, (2005): 25–30.

Espinoza Fernández, J. 'Evolución constitucional de la regulación de la energía'. In *Regulación del sector energético.* 1997, 51–70.

Foucher, Sam. 'An Update on Mexico's Oil Production: The Rapid Collapse of Cantarell by the Numbers' (31 January 2007). The Oil Drum, available at www-.theoildrum .com.
Garza, R. *El derecho Mexicano de la explotación petrolera y los contratos de burgos.*2005, available at www.itesm.mx.
Gersherson, A. 'Hechos históricos importantes del petróleo en México', in *El petróleo en la historia y la cultura de México*, ed. José Alfonso Suarez, 2008.
González Márquez, J. J. & Montelongo Buenavista, I. *El Nuevo Derecho Ambiental Mexicano. México.* Biblioteca de Ciencias Sociales y Humanidades, Universidad Autónoma Metropolitana, 1997.
González Márquez, José Juan & Montelongo Buenavista, Ivette. *Introducción al Derecho Ambiental Mexicano. México.* Library of Social Sciences and Humanities, Universidad Autónoma Metropolitana, Series Law, 1999.
González Márquez, José Juan. 'Algunas consideraciones preliminares sobre el régimen jurídico de la responsabilidad por el daño ambiental en México'. In *La responsabilidad por el daño ambiental.* Serie de documentos sobre derecho ambiental, N° 5. Programa de las Naciones Unidas para el Medio Ambiente (PNUMA). Oficina Regional para América Latina y el Caribe (ORPALC). Ciudad de México, México, 1996, 389–456.
González Márquez, José Juan. 'Origen, concepto y contenido del derecho ambiental'. In *Revista Mexicana de Legislación Ambiental*, publicación revista cuatrimestral mayo-diciembre 2002, año3, número 9 y 10, 5–28.
González Márquez, José Juan. 'La configuración del Derecho Ambiental como disciplina autónoma'. In *Los retos del Derecho Ambiental en México*, edited by de Revuelta Vaquero Benjamín. México, 2010, 17–32.
González Márquez, José Juan. *Teoría del derecho ambiental, los fundamentos jurídicos de la sostenibilidad, volumen 1.* Instituto Mexicano de Investigaciones en Derecho Ambiental A.C., México. 2011.
González Márquez, José Juan. *La naturaleza jurídica de la Evaluación del Impacto Ambiental. Análisis de Derecho Comparado.* Instituto Mexicano de Investigaciones en Derecho Ambiental A.C., México. 2010.
GWEC. *Global Wind 2005 Report*, available at www.gwec.net, 34–35.
Hernández Peñaloza, A. *Bases para una política petrolera de México alternativa al modelo neoliberal: contribución al Segundo Diálogo Nacional para un nuevo Proyecto de Nación* (February 5, 2005), available at http://www.iie.org.mx/boletin042003/inv.pdf.
Huacuz, J. 'Energías renovables: ¿opción real para la generación eléctrica en México?'. *Boletín del Instituto de Investigaciones Eléctricas* 111, Number 1 (2003), available at www.iie.org.mx.
Jiménez, R. 'Elementos históricos para la interpretación del régimen constitucional del petróleo de los mexicanos'. In *El petróleo en la historia de la cultura de México*, edited by José Alfonso Suarez. 2008.
Koyama, K. 'Prospects for International Oil Market and Crude Oil Prices in 2007' (15 December 2005), available at eneken.iee.or.jp.
Enrique, L. *Saber ambiental.* México, siglo, 1998 XXI.

Prieur, M. *Droit de l'environnement*. Paris: Dalloz, 1999. Evaluación de Impacto Ambiental Transfronteriza en Centroamérica, Lineamientos Generales Grethel Aguilar, Alejandro Iza y Marianela Cedeño.

Martin, Mateo R. *New Instruments for the Environmental Tutelage*. 1994.

Memorias del Congreso realizado por la Comisión de Ecología y Medio Ambiente de la Cámara de Diputados del Congreso de la Unión y la Universidad Juárez Autónoma de Tabasco, sobre: El petróleo y su impacto en la ecología, Tabasco, México, 16–18 Oct. 1996.

Panorama general de la Seguridad Social en México, available at www.indetec.gob.mx.

Peeters, M. 'European Climate Change: Critical Issues and Change for the Future'. In *Yearbook of International Environmental Law*, edited by Ale Kustian Fauchald & Jacob Weksman. 2005, 185.

Programa GEI México, available at www.geimexico.org.

Quintana Valtierra J. *Derecho Ambiental Mexicano, lineamientos generales*. Editorial Porrúa, México, 2000.

'Reforma Energética. Iniciativa para fortalecer PEMEX'. 2008, available at www.pemex.com.

Secretaria de Energía, available at http://www.energia.gob.mx/.

Secretaría de Energía-GTZ. *Energías renovables para el desarrollo sustentable en México 2009*, available at http://plataforma.responsable.net/explorar/energias-renovables-para-desarrollo-sustentable-mexico-0.

Serrano J.L.. *Principios de Derecho Ambiental y Ecología Jurídica*. España. Editorial Trotta, 2007.

Tzbi, M. *Ideología y praxis política de Lázaro Cárdenas*. 9th edn. 1982, 195.

White House Office of Communications. *Twenty in Ten: Straightening America's Energy Security* (1 February 2007), available at http://www.energy.gov/downloads/twenty-ten-strengthening-americas-energy-security.

Wionczek, M. & Ragaei E. El Mallakh. *Mexico's Energy Resources: Toward a Policy of Diversification*. 1985.

'World Fossil Fuels Consumption per Source, 1950–1988 (in Million of Tons Oil Equivalent)', available at people.hofstra.edu.

Selected Bibliography

Index

The numbers here refer to paragraph numbers.

Index

www.ingramcontent.com/pod-product-compliance
Ingram Content Group UK Ltd.
Pitfield, Milton Keynes, MK11 3LW, UK
UKHW020144290926
15471UKWH00004B/692

9 789403 516462